KALEIDOSCOPE

An Eclectic Collection

KALEIDOSCOPE

An Eclectic Collection

From Family Worship Center Academy
Pueblo, Colorado

Edited by Charissa Fryberger

Kha'ris Expressions
Beulah, Colorado
2024

Front Cover Design by Luis Dante Munoz

Front Cover photo credits:

Charissa Fryberger: Cross, Multnomah Bridge, Cat, and Rose Garden

David Fryberger: Mountain scene

Uhooep: Saling ship https://commons.wikimedia.org/w/index.php?search=sailing+ship&title=Special:MediaSearch&go=Go&type=image

Safa Daneshvar: Hermit Crab https://commons.wikimedia.org/w/index.php?search=Hermit+crab&title=Special:MediaSearch&go=Go&type=image

Beni Ziegler: Wolf and bear https://www.flickr.com/photos/zieglerbeni/albums

Wikimedia: WWII Tank https://commons.wikimedia.org/w/index.php?search=WWI+tank&title=Special:MediaSearch&go=Go&type=image

Petr Kratochvil: Latte https://commons.wikimedia.org/w/index.php?search=table+with+coffee&title=Special:MediaSearch&go=Go&type=image

Hubble Telescope: Stars https://esahubble.org/images/potw1804a/

SCRIPTURE CITATIONS

English Standard Version (ESV): The Holy Bible, English Standard Version. ESV® Text Edition: 2016. Copyright © 2001 by Crossway Bibles, a publishing ministry of Good News Publishers.

New King James Version (NKJV): Scripture taken from the New King James Version®. Copyright © 1982 by Thomas Nelson.

TABLE OF CONTENTS

TABLE OF CONTENTS

FICTION

POETRY

TABLE OF CONTENTS

TABLE OF CONTENTS

ESSAYS AND COMMENTARY

Forward

Ranging from wildly fantastical to introspective; from inspirational to experiential; from sacred to secular; and from poetic to just the facts, the pieces presented in this book offer glimpses into the hearts, minds, imaginations, and experiences of the students, parents, teachers, pastors, and supporters of Family Worship Center Academy as they live out their lives and their faith in the swirling cultural waters of 2023-2024.

Some of the contributors whose work populates these pages are children; others are teens, working adults, or senior citizens. Together, their eclectic writings form a colorful kaleidoscope of ideas. They offer their thoughts, memories, dreams, fears, and fantasies as a unique snapshot in the ever-changing, ever-growing mosaics of their lives.

Surely such a book published last year or next year or five years from now would present a different image, as the complex patterns of their experiences and understandings continue to move and swirl, incessantly bending their reflections through and around each other. For now, I hope you will enjoy the varying moods, styles, and colors of these interwoven thoughts, as you view this kaleidoscope through their eyes.

--Charissa Fryberger

LIFE STORIES

Hide and Seek

By Abbey Hawn

I remember a little game I loved to play when I was a preschooler. It was kind of like hide and seek, only, instead of actually hiding, I would just cover my eyes with my hands. In my little mind, I figured, "If I can't see them, then they can't see me!" I was always quite puzzled when, after a few seconds, they said they still could.

Eventually, I realized that my eyes are a very small part of my body. Even though covering them hid the whole world from me, I still remained quite visible. The ability for someone to see me was completely independent of whether or not I could see them. Just because I hindered my own eyes didn't mean I hindered theirs.

Over time, I also realized that it's the same way with the Lord. Sometimes in life, I can't see Him, and I assume that I must also be hidden from His sight. However, I have begun to understand that, just like when I played hide and seek as a little child, my ability to see Him does not have any bearing on His ability to see me.

He is the God who sees (Gen 16), and my perspective (or lack of it!) doesn't affect that at all. His eyes are ever upon me, whether my eyes are covered or gazing directly at Him. In the times when I feel noticed and the times when I don't, He is always there, looking right at me with unhindered eyes. I can have confidence that in each and every season, my Father sees me, even when I can't see Him. And just like with my little game, I know that one day my eyes *will* be uncovered to see Him, and I will then know with more assurance than ever, that He really was watching me all along.

Slobber Monster

By Kara (AK) Evans

Age 15

When I was younger, my brothers and I played a goofy game called Slobber Monster that came from a video game called *Skylanders*. My older brother and I got to a level in the game where dog-like creatures that had slobber coming out of their mouths attacked us; we called them Slobber Monsters.

We loved this level and played it over and over again just because of those creatures. My little brother, who was about two, often sat and watched us play. He was too young to play video games with us (though he really wanted to), so we came up with a way of playing it without the video game. That way he wouldn't feel left out.

We pretended that he was the Slobber Monster and we ran away from him. He thought it was so much fun to chase us around! He sometimes even grabbed small toys and waved them in the air as he chased us. It was so amazing for my big brother and I to see the joy light up my little brother's face as he ran growling after his older siblings while we yelled in mock fear!

We played this game almost daily. It is one of my favorite memories of my brothers and I playing together because my little brother is adopted, and this was one of the games we played while we were still fostering him. It was a great way for us to bond.

Over the years we made this game subtly more complicated. After a while, we stopped playing it. It became merely a memory, but a wonderful memory all the same. All three of us grew closer when we spent time playing games like this together. This is one of the things from our childhood that we still reminisce about to this day. Every time we do so, we can't help but smile at the memory.

Lucky

By Amy Munoz

Age 15

My dad left to go to the store one day when we lived in Arkansas. For some reason, he came back a few minutes later. He came inside and said, "I have a surprise for all of you!" My mom, my brother, my friend, and I came out running. My dad opened the trunk of his truck to show us a cute, little pit bull puppy! She was white with light brown spots on her back. We took her inside and fed her milk.

My dad told us where he had found her. This may be shocking, but she was left next to a highway. We were surprised that a person could just leave her like that. She could have been killed by a car. Later on that day, we went to the store, and we were all discussing what name would fit the pit bull. My dad suggested, "We should name her Lucky."

I quickly said, "That name fits perfectly because she could have been killed, but she was saved!" So, we all agreed to it. Lucky was an obedient dog. She followed any command my dad gave her. She was a sweetheart!

In Arkansas, we had racoons around, often getting into trash cans. My mom's brother visited us one day and heard Lucky growling and crying out in the backyard (my mom never allowed pets inside the house). The next day, we couldn't find Lucky. My uncle told my parents about what he'd heard. The only thing I heard was my parents calling her name, "Lucky, where are you?!"

That day, my neighbor came over to our house to play with my brother and I. She asked me what had happened, but I didn't know. My mom told the three of us not to go outside. We went anyway, just to see what was going on. We found Lucky up front near the door, looking for my parents.

I was horrified by what had happened to her. She had been attacked by a racoon. She had no nose, her right back leg was chewed off, a piece of her ear was bitten, and most of her tail was gone. My dad took her to the vet, and despite her injuries, she started healing really well.

When the time came for us to move to Pueblo, my brother and I came home from school to play with her, but she was gone. I was heartbroken when I couldn't find her. I ask my mom where she was. She told me, "Your dad took Lucky to a ranch where they will take good care of her because we can't take her to Pueblo with us. We had no time to say goodbye. I still miss her a lot. Lucky was a really good girl. Lucky<3

Take This Child…

By Pat Gyger

"Take this child and nurse him for me, and I will give you your wages…"

--Exodus 2:9

When we think of the above Bible verse, we think of someone like a nurse tending to the *physical* needs of another, but the dictionary definition goes even further. It defines the verb "to nurse" as: "to look after carefully as to promote growth, development, etc.; foster, cherish." With that definition in mind, I want to share with you the following story:

Once upon a time in a church, there was a man who taught children. Since the church was small, the teacher had children of various ages in his class. One day, they discussed the term "togetherness" in class. A question was raised as to its meaning. Wanting to give the children an example, the teacher stated that when you do anything together with your family that tends to draw the family closer, that's called, "togetherness." He then asked, "How many of you do anything together with your family?" To his amazement, not a single hand was raised.

Having grown up in a family where the teacher

himself did not experience "togetherness," that became very important to him. He decided right then to give these children the "togetherness" he had never had. He would give them one evening every two weeks when those who could, would meet and do things together. They would call it "Fun Night." Sometimes they played ball; sometimes they went on a picnic or went fishing; sometimes they just sat around a bonfire roasting marshmallows, eager to share what was on their minds as the teacher carefully listened. The kids loved the teacher because he showed an interest in *them* and what they were doing, and there wasn't a single kid who preferred to stay home, sitting in front of the computer or TV when they knew they were going on an activity planned *just for them.*

The teacher made sure to invite the dads along, especially when they were going on fishing outings or camping trips. He wanted the dads to experience the joy that rightly belonged to them. The teacher knew you couldn't put a price on that.

Even though he was a teacher, he said that he had never learned how to adequately tell a little girl that it was time to go home—a girl who had never had the pleasure of holding a fishing pole in all of her twelve years; a girl who hadn't had a nibble in two hours and, yet, wanted to stay on, begging, "Please, can't we stay a little longer?"

And, how could the teacher refuse a boy who asked the same night, "Will you take me fishing again in the morning?" The teacher knew the boy would be leaving town in three days, and he would never again have the opportunity to spend time with the boy. So, the teacher agreed to pick up the boy at 4:30 a.m., a time of the *boy's* choosing. When the teacher arrived, he found out that the boy had been up since 3:00 a.m., impatiently waiting.

These may seem like small incidents to some, but they made for unforgettable memories, not only for the children, but also for the teacher.

This teacher "nursed" the children. He promoted growth and development as he fostered and cherished them. He taught the children by example that each one was precious in God's sight, and that a Godly man is a man of his word.

Exodus 2:9 also speaks about wages, but the teacher would tell you that what little time he actually spent with the children had been repaid to him many times over in wages of love, wages that truly belonged to the parents. The teacher knew that parents could reap those "paydays" for themselves, if they would only "Take this child and nurse him."

The teacher's friends all called him, "Koke," but I called him Dad.

Don't Try This at Home!

By Devlyn Woodall

Age 13

My friend and I were messing around with the seatbelts in the van one night. I wrapped mine around my neck—twice. Then it happened…the mechanism locked! I was losing air! I was yelling, but no sound came out.

I woke up in the street with the first responders looking over me. I was rushed to the ER with a "severe strangulation wound." My face was purple and swollen and my eyes were black. Later, I found out that everyone who was there when it happened thought I had died.

I had been five to eight minutes without oxygen. I was dead.

But now I'm alive.

Pretending
to Know What You're Doing

By Donna Ford Ferrell

I Tim 1:7 says, "God has not given us a spirit of fear, but of power and of love and of a sound mind (NKJV)." My story is one of having no fear and tackling the unknown.

When my kids hit high school, I wanted to watch out for them, so I asked the editor of the Chaffee County Times, "Can I be your sports reporter for Buena Vista High School?"

My first football game was a venture into the unknown, as I had never even watched a football game. I didn't even like football, but my son loved the game. I went into Coach Sacco's classroom after the first game and said, "I have some good news, and I have some bad news." He asked for the bad news first, so I told him that I had never watched a football game, but the good news was that I was the new sports reporter for the local newspaper. There was an audible groan and a look of disbelief on the Coach's face.

So began my new career. To get my stories right, I

often had to ask my husband to read them and correct the mistakes. "No, Donna, they are going toward the goal, not that way."

It was hard standing on the sidelines and hearing kids take hits. The impact was sometimes loud. Then there was the camera. Taking shots of football is not easy. I had to guess where the pass would go and take a picture of what could happen. One day I was on the sideline, focused thru the lens of the camera, and I heard "He's coming around the end." I looked up and saw our leading runner barreling toward me carrying the football with at least six big bruisers chasing him. I turned and ran, but the school had strung a wire across my path to keep people out of the area. I crashed into the wire and went down. The runner crashed right behind me, and they helped him up. Me, I crawled under the wire, glad to be alive. No one noticed.

The next day I asked the runner, "Do you have a linc across your chest?"

"How did you know?" he asked.

"I have one also." My clipboard also had numerous cleat marks on it where the players had run right over it.

Then there was the time I was covering a game in Leadville at 10,000 feet, and it was snowing. Cold, mercy me, it was cold. Then my camera froze. I had to put it in my armpit to thaw it out. Now that is a shock to the system.

Early in my son's football career, he rode home with us after a game in Florence. It took a long time because in the 90-mile trip, he threw up 19 times. He was a freshman playing varsity and wanted to do it perfectly, so his nerves made him ill every game. Finally, one coach suggested that his mother had found that if she made him macaroni and cheese before the games, it would settle his stomach. Guess what? It worked. We did four years with macaroni and cheese before every game.

Another time our team played a team from a Christian school in Colorado Springs. My son came up to me and said, "Mom, they are so dirty. They cuss and use the Lord's name in vain. They even spit on us when they tackle us." I went over to the other side and ask to "interview" the coach and confronted him with the disrespect. After the half time break, there was no more disrespect or using God's name as a cuss word. I think there was some soul searching during the half time talk.

Then there was Alamosa. We played them during my son's senior year. They had not lost a game—and we beat them by 2 points! Their only loss that year! During the game, my camera and I went over on the Alamosa side to take pictures. The Alamosa athletic director came down and told me I couldn't be on that side of the field, so I stayed. He called the police. When they arrived, the police asked our athletic director if he could do something with me, and his answer was, "No, even her own husband can't do anything with her." The police laughed and left. I stayed on the Alamosa side throughout the game because the light was behind me, and it made better photos (even when I ran out of film). And reporters *are* allowed to be on either side.

I learned to understand the game and could write a story with the team heading the correct way down the field, even though taking pictures of gymnastics and track was a lot more fun—and the weather was better. But I was the one cheering when my son, as a senior, played his last football game.

My Little Angel

By Marissa Miller

Age 15

Chapter 1: Tired

When talking about something dark, deep, or upsetting, what is the reaction of the people around? I'll bet that it is uncomfortable for both parties. Normally, talking about those topics, can change the way others see us. It's because it's a glimpse of how we really think—stuff a person often can't say because they can't find the words. It's as if their mouths can't come up with the words on the spot.

A good majority of the people who I've known wanted to hear what I thought about life, which I find sad...real. That's life. But they get sensitive when they hear it—like they don't want to believe that, like something's wrong with me. People want to know my take on life, until I say something that they don't like. Then they refuse to listen further. They ignore the signs. Even my dad doesn't want to hear about it. He especially doesn't want to hear about times when I've thought of running, because he says I have a "great life." It's frustrating, knowing that talking about something aggressive or even giving a general opinion will end in some form of war—a war that doesn't need to be physical to be considered such.

What's inside will eventually attract attention on the outside. Nobody is strong enough to hide their real feelings forever.

*****

"Your dad's gonna be here any minute! Are you ready??" I can hear my mom shout from her bedroom, which is only one room away. Recently, she's been diagnosed with heart failure. Every day feels worse than the last for her. Her health affects me in ways I can't really explain. I care about her, I really do, but when her health starts feeling like an anvil getting close above my head, I try to care…less.

Is that wrong?

I realize I've been sitting here writing for so long that I haven't even gotten ready for school.

"Can I just…stay home…?" I groan.

"Why?" she asks, as if she doesn't know all that I deal with in my own life.

"I'm not feeling up to it." I know I won't be able to stay home, but it's always worth a shot, right? Maybe mental health days will become more common in my family.

"It's coming up on the end of the year. Plus, you know your daddy won't let you stay. Come on!" she shouts. I get out of bed, throwing myself together and doing the bare minimum for getting ready. I really only go to school for my friends now. Nothing else interests me anymore. I used to be a gifted child, believe it or not: straight A's, good health, great friends, good teachers. But now I've 'lost my spark' I guess. I'm still talented, or so I'm told, but anyone can say that to me five hundred times, and I'm not gonna personally believe it.

What was my dream about? I do the last of my things and walk out the door. *I thought it was a good one. Had to have been if I can't even manage to wake up enough today.* I walk out to my dad waiting outside to take me to school. Once I get into his vehicle, we say the same things we do every school day.

"Morning."

"Nnh.."

Then, the rest of the drive is with music; he's talking, but I'm not listening. I don't mean to, I swear. I love his stories. He's funny, but he can be an ******

28

sometimes too. *Did I really just call him that? Lord, I don't mean that...* I realize, glancing over at him, that he seems to have stopped talking. I decide to stay quiet for the rest of the drive. Getting to school, I step out of the vehicle, grabbing my stuff.

"Have a good day," he says. "Love you. Be safe."

"I won't. Love you too," I reply, knowing he thinks that "not having a good day" or "not being safe" is a joke when… I know that I mean it. Nothing is a good day anymore. I shut the door carefully, so that he doesn't get upset by me slamming it. He never has gotten mad at that, but sometimes things just click in his head.

I take a step into the school, and a weight places itself on my shoulders, adding to the weight of my backpack and the stress I carry from everything else. I sign in, set my stuff down, and stay by the door to watch the people walking inside like a line of ants going to their little dirt pile of a home. One of the pastors walks in. "What's up!" he cheers.

"Tired," I say in response, seeing the light fade in his eyes. He tilts his head only slightly.

"Didn't get enough sleep?" he asks.

"No." *Because of how much this world sucks and because of my slipping grades and this religion that I don't understand...*

*****

I wake up. Well, not "wake up." I snap back into reality, but so much time has passed. Math, my first real class after chapel, just ended. *What happened!?* I panic, rushing to grab my stuff as people are trying to walk by. I'm just in the way, like always. My mouth moves to talk to my friends who are waiting for me, but my thoughts don't let me process what I'm saying at all. It's as if my mouth had a mind of its own rather than my body's mind. I catch up to the ones leaving and wait for our next class to start.

"Gym class! Let's go!" my teacher shouts as I'm filling my water bottle. I look at the restrooms, thinking about skipping but knowing I can't do that… I walk out with my little group.

"Hey. Hey!" One of them waves their hand in front of me, making me flinch. "Dawg, where are you today…?"

"I'm here…—"

"Hey!" a man calls out. I stop. When I turn, I see the pastor from earlier. I tilt my head, and he signals me over.

"Oooh, someone's in trouble," one of my friends says, nearly sending me into a panic attack simply thinking of that possibility. *Do they know that kind of crap actually hurts..?* I roll my eyes, trying to play it off as I walk over toward the pastor.

"What…" I say in a near groan.

"You looked so tired this morning, and I was thinking about your answer to me."

I panic. *I didn't tell him that very rude bit earlier, did I?! What did I say!?* "Uhh, remind me what I said again...?"

"You told me you didn't get enough sleep from stress."

...I don't know what I thought I said, but that wasn't it. "Right."

"So are you… good?"

"Stress is normal."

"But it's not good if you aren't sleeping."

"If it becomes bothersome, I'll get a therapist. M'kay?"

The rest of the conversation is a blur. He walks away. I hear, "Hey! Get down to the field for gym!"

Next thing I know, I'm at the field, but I'm not up to running any laps. I walk them with a few classmates. Then the gym teacher calls out that it's a free day to do whatever we want after doing these laps. I sigh in relief, knowing that we aren't doing anything else.

My mind spaces the rest of P.E. out. It's a Monday, so we have science, or biology. I don't care. Why change the name when the stuff we learn is the same as third grade, when it was just science? I sit down and end up drawing in class to keep to myself and my own thoughts. I feel a presence over my shoulder.

"Do you want to draw your little pictures elsewhere

or pay attention to the class?" I ignore him. "Put your sketchbook away and pay attention, learn something—"

"I already know this stuff. Leave me alone!" Again, I come back to reality where he's just waiting. I throw down my book with panic already setting in. *Why can't they get it? Do they want me to panic, then vomit from it? I swear, I'm gonna lose it with this school.* I get lost in thought as these things repeat in my head. Luckily that basically means I'm mentally skipping class, and now it's lunch.

I don't eat anything. The smell makes something in me turn. Lunch becomes boring.

"Are you gonna eat?" a lunch lady asks.

No, I'm gonna throw up if I eat this food. I come back in my head"...I'm not hungry," is my actual reply.

I come to remember my father being the reason I don't speak out. *"You just have to bite your tongue and get through it."* His voice echoes through the chambers of my mind.

"Are you sure?" she asks. I nod my head, making a petty face just because I want her to go away. "Okay…" She turns and leaves.

What happened to my life. I've lost enough weight, and I continue to not eat. I don't understand it. I want to continue what I was writing this morning before leaving. Writing and drawing are what I want to do, but it's not like this place helps. Only one class is trying to help. People wonder why I love that class so much. They complain about a lot of homework, but I'm okay, because I enjoy writing.

I come back and realize a whole class has gone by. My last class is beginning, and I make it in late. People just watch me as I sit down. I end up drawing for the rest of this class, too, and not listening to this politics and crap I don't care about anymore. I wait for my dad to pick me up and walk out once I see his light blue headlights coming towards the school. He parks, and I quickly hop in.

"How was your day?" he asks, just trying to be nice, I'm sure.

"Boring. I wanna get out of here."

"Right. Well…" He begins to pull out of the parking lot. "My day, believe it or not, was full of kids just puking their guts out."

Here we go again… I get that he's a custodian and all, but is that all he does? There has to be something better…

"There's a stomach bug going around and they were all th—w—g -p. —zy d-y…" His voice fades out of my hearing. I can't listen to his stories right now. Maybe tomorrow. Fifteen minutes later, we're in my driveway and walking into the house. I put my shoes up and walk straight through the kitchen to the doorway to the living room, bedrooms, and bathroom. I go straight down the hall to my room. I throw my bag down, falling into bed.

Finally, home. I rest a bit before grabbing what I was writing this morning.

Survival can be seen in many ways—survive a sickness, survive through a shootout in a local Walmart, or survive a real-life knife fight. Those are all fights that need to be overcome to move on. The thing that nobody talks about though, is the fight that goes on inside that turns to hell and shuts down a person from the inside out. I think that mental fights are some of the most dangerous and damaging, and people forget that. They are dangerous because they're different for every person going through them. We can't help a person with an issue if we have no idea what their level of problems is.

I know that I am one of many who are in danger from their own thoughts. Thoughts that can feel like a virus with no cure; thoughts that shorten my breath and cause changes in... everything.

I understand that only I can change myself, which is why I don't change. This war inside of my head distracts me from the necessities that I need to correct this error in my brain. A "flaw in my code," perhaps. I do wish that I could have stopped it earlier, but it felt like I had no choice because of these things that come up out of the depths of my soul and pull my mentality into a place where I can't change myself the way I know I should. I have no time to focus on my own needs with other burdens traveling around my mind. I think that they need me, these people in my life who I feel I can't let go of. My own Anxiety tells me that, which is why Depression and Anxiety can't get along.

Chapter 2: Meet the Emotions

"We're nothing. We'll always be nothing, and everyone knows it. They'll forget us in a week, just give up."

"NO! The weight will be on our friends—"

"Our?"

"We'll be a burden to them! We can't leave that for them. We care too much!"

"More of a burden than we already are? We already lay explanations about mommy health on people. Seems like a contribution, no?"

"Whose fault is that? You just vent and vent when you should be shutting your mouth—"

"Could you two cut it out already…" I groan, communicating in my mind with these two emotions who are always arguing in my head and keeping me from thinking straight.

Meet Depression, my buzz–kill, my thought–drain, my reason for thinking of leaving everything behind. Then, Anxiety, my fear… but worse than fear. Anxiety tears my mind apart, stubborn but still caring. Depression wants nothing to do with the people around me; Anxiety says that I need them to function, as if I haven't pushed them away or ignored them by accident. These two represent two very different ways to describe any relationship I have, yet I have no idea which one is true.

They argue back and forth, on and on. The talking, or rather, the shouting at each other causes a ringing in my ears that I can't manage to shake no matter how much I try. When they start, they don't stop. So, I sleep it off with music blasting in my earbuds to tame them both. Of course, then I miss out on life.

After I write my thoughts, I fall asleep. I sleep and sleep, sometimes through dinner, waking up at 2:00 am and regretting it all.

"We can just keep sleeping, come on. It's better when we sleep," Depression starts.

"Are you crazy—" Anxiety replies, fueling the fire of an argument.

"Yes."

"Shut the hell up. Hngh… We can't just continue to miss out on life like this. The loved ones might not need her, but they want her! Why can't you see that she can make people smile and laugh if we just… give her the chance." Anxiety shoves depression into the wall of my mind, leaving a mark, a scar on my brain that will cause me to think about this for the next few days.

"Why can't *you* see that she can't do this anymore??" Depression fires back, "She's tired, and you push her. If you keep pushing her, she will fail on her own, moron. She may end up sick just like her mother."

Suddenly, Anxiety spikes, torn as to how to take that comment, and leaving me, the host, to feel even worse. Now I'm torn as well. I focus on the deafening sound of these voices in my mind pulling me in every direction until my mind is torn apart and rearranged in every wrong way. I believe this is the way any mental disorders I have started. It causes my mind to not work properly anymore. I get confused and lose touch with reality.

Then a new voice pipes up. "Let's go off on someone. It's easy, and trust me, very fun. This voice is always violent, a crazy, malfunctioning version of me: Anger.

"It'll feel worse if we do nothing," says another voice. "I know…how about that teacher who makes her so pissed that she wants to say something rude, but as long as Silence does her job, she'll never get that out to help her mental state. She'll never cry for help. Just nothing. Absolutely nothing. It's not like anyone cares enough to help anyway."

I call the one speaking, Harm. Or Self–Harm, but Harm feels like a better description because it's not only me it wants to hurt. Harm wants to damage everyone around me. Even though I can't see this emotion, I can feel it—and that petty smile that comes with. The only way I'm allowed to let Anger out is physically, until I'm bruised, bleeding, or worse.

Silence keeps my trap shut and stitched together so that I can't call for help. This gives Harm more power. Together, the voices make sure that Harm can take the reins and give advice on how to make the situation worse. And from there, Anger and Silence team up to push people away and manipulate people under Harm's control. Their conversations often sound like three torturers planning for their next persecution.

Another day feels like another day in Hell. It's only Tuesday and I dread every second of the day as well as the rest of the week. I'm so tired that I just want to stay home and do nothing at all; just lay down and stare at the ceiling while I rot. The school that I'm in is Christ–based, and my dad believes that because of that, it's a good school, but nothing feels safe there, and they don't help me with my faith. The world has gone so much to **** that not even God's house makes me feel even okay anymore.

"If she continues to cuss, she won't even make it into Heaven. We aren't even worthy of that," Depression comments.

"I… don't think that's how that works? Is it?" Anxiety replies, speeding up my pulse as a reaction to feeling like there is going to be nothing better.

"No, but we've done a lot of things that wouldn't get us in," Harm scoffs.

These thoughts get me through my last class. Hell, it gets me through the rest of the week. I don't think about anything from school, and it just passes by. That's exactly what I've been doing with life as well. It sucks but… I can't help it. I'm missing out on my years and nothing can be done.

The next few days are exactly the same as the last. Isn't that the definition of insanity? I remember from a long time ago in middle school—something about…

"Following a ritual and expecting a different outcome?"

"Damn—school is actually driving us insane," Anger says and laughs.

Either way it's no fun for me.

It becomes the end of Thursday, packing up and leaving to go to a home that doesn't feel like home anymore. It feels more like a place for the night, as if I've been wandering Earth for hours, and this is the only place I can go to rest before the next day. I first walk into the bathroom. I look in the mirror, thinking. My mom barges in at random, making me jump. "WHAT??"

"I've been calling you! Don't shout at me either! I swear you're just someone else now!"

"This is how I talk."

"No, I hear someone else."

I freeze at her words. I can't take it, so I leave, heading towards my room and nearly slamming the door. *How can I feel sorry for her when she says things like that to me?* I fall onto my bed and drop my bag and lunchbox, adding to what my parents would call my "Depression Room." I never thought that I would come to the point where the shower feels miles away and the trash can and vacuum even further. As I lay in bed, I look down at my floor, seeing that same piece of trash and cat–hairball–looking crap still on my floor from weeks ago.

I think about getting up, but I'm paralyzed. My legs feel chained to the bed, and I can't physically do anything about it. Then my mind loses track of what I wanted to do in the first place, so I give up and let my bad consume me and my spirit. My mind races for no reason and my heart begins to speed up because I feel claustrophobic, but I know that I'm not. I can't be in such a state when I'm in a totally open room, right? Or is it the mess that fuels that feeling?

I feel overwhelmed, even though I have nothing to be overwhelmed about. None of this crap in my mind is mine, and I don't know why or where it came from.

I'm stuck.

I pick up my phone and realize there were assignments in nearly all my classes, but I don't know exactly what they were. I think about how disappointed everyone will be because of my terrible grades, and I wonder what will happen if I don't keep my GPA over 2.0; it's currently at a 2.03.

I drop my phone on my pounding chest. It's like my chest is a locked door, and my heart is the person I locked out. It's banging and banging.

"What if we had a heart attack right here?" Anxiety asks. I know that's me worrying about whether my mother's heart failure could be passed to me.

"Painful way to go. What a coincidence that would be, but she would be out of everyone's way at least," Depression replies, calm, as usual, even in stupid situations.

Can everyone just SHUT UP!? I shout in my mind.

"Damn, sorry." Anger says very sarcastically, chuckling at me and everyone else arguing in my head. I can't even manage to do anything about them right now. I just give up and start trying to drift off to sleep.

I wake to my alarm, a guitar solo to "Sweet Child O' Mine" by Guns N' Roses. It's for 10:00pm—to clean my new piercing. I turn off the alarm, but I still can't get up, so I end up drifting back into sleep. The piercing can wait. Things just always wait. That's how it works in such a mindset, until I realize how much stuff has been waiting, and I know I need to do something about it.

Next thing I know, I've slept off the whole weekend. I wake to my school morning alarm. *♪It was the heat of the moment. Telling me what my heart meant! The heat of the moment, showed in your eyes~♪*— I turn it off and sit up, confused. It was just Friday, and now I'm waking back up on Monday without any break at all. My homework isn't even done, like I know what it even was. I know Depression set me up for that one. I start to get up so I can rush to get ready. Maybe I'll have time to do something for homework. But as I start to get up, something holds me back. I'm still holding onto the bed, not by free will.

I groan, and give up, shutting my eyes and ending up in my dad's truck, as if time just passed by, and I forgot everything else I did before getting to the front of my house. I look around as if I had just passed out and am in a daze. He's talking, but I don't know what he's saying. He soon drops me off at school again.

"Adios, have a good day. Love you."

"Love you too." I muster up a smile and close the door, walking inside. Just like usual, I space out with the weight on my shoulders clinging to me like it's a parasite, and I'm its only chance at survival.

The day goes as usual… Someone asks how my weekend was, but I can't remember. The conversation moves on, until I hear something. Someone.

I make out a small voice calling my name. I look around. Nobody said a thing. "Did you call me?" I ask a friend who's nearby. It was a girl's voice. I just know it.

"No? Are you alright? Haha!"

"Yeah. Just thought I heard my name…"

While my friend can move on, the moment replays in my head for a while, until I groan, rubbing my head and letting the day pass me by. All these teachers just continue to call on me and pick on me for things I don't know the answer to. It goes on and on. I zone out until the end of school. I wish I could just stay in a zone–out state. I know that no person can do that forever though.

Suddenly I hear it again. "Hey!" I flinch, looking around again. The confusion on my face just grows. Nobody is looking at me as if they are talking to me, but that sounded… right in my ear. At least I thought so. I say goodbye to a few of my friends and get home, thinking about what I keep hearing. The problem is that I'm not the only confused one. Every emotion—all of them in my mind—they're just as befuddled.

"Weird. Hey, who's messing around??" Anger asks the rest.

"Dude, we're in the same room…" Depression replies.

"At least we know Silence didn't do it, haha!!" Harm jokes, even though I have known Silence to have a voice as well, almost like a literal version of the saying, "The silence is so loud…"

While they debate and soon argue, I can't figure it out either.

What is happening??

Chapter 3: Trust

♪*It was the heat of the moment. Telling me what my heart meant—*♪

"Hngh…" I sit up in bed. "It's only Tuesday…" I groan, stretching and slowly getting up. I realize that I have actually gotten up this time. Shaking it off, I get ready for the day. Something is different, and I'm not sure what it is.

I am ready on time and waiting for my dad rather than him waiting for me. When he pulls up, I have all my things; I've even made time for extra things such as actually managing to take care of myself. I've done my hair, brushed my teeth, put on makeup, and put on an outfit that hasn't been rushed. I've thought through what I needed for the day. I smile and wave at my dad before getting in.

"Morning!"

"Morning? Hah, you're lively, and dressed up like you didn't just roll out of bed. What's the occasion?"

"No occasion."

"...Alright—anyways. I'm happy that you're starting off better than I am. These teachers had me all over the place this morning." He explains, talking about his work as a custodian. He puts the truck in gear to begin making the drive for school. For once, we talk, like the way we used to. I really listen to him this time. When we arrive at school, I miss him after getting out of his truck and waving before watching him drive off. Walking into school wasn't so bad, really. I enter, and a friend greets me, so we talk.

"I'm tired," she says, sitting down on the floor.

"I feel fine today, actually."

"Lucky for you. You're never like that."

"Shut up—" I sit next to her and we watch people come in. I manage to greet the people who walk by with a smile for once. *What's happening right now? Why did I all of a sudden become...outgoing?* It's not like it's a bad thing, just surprising. To me and, apparently, to everyone around me.

Chappel goes smoothly. Math is the same as usual, but with more laughter. *Am I causing this joy?* I ask myself, feeling a little bit proud. P.E. goes well because it's a free day. We all love those anyway. Everything is going well, until…it's time to go to the class I dislike the most. I feel uneasy about this class, but I'm gonna stick it out, and if anything, I'm gonna make it fun. We take our seats with me in the front next to a guy I really don't talk to much. I hear the voices in my head talking in confusion, then arguing, but I tune them out this time. They aren't gonna ruin this day.

The class starts out okay, but it is too good to last. I'm not listening, then suddenly I hear the teacher focusing on the boy behind me. He's my friend, well, more like a brother. He's funny. Really, all of us love his personality. The teacher is scolding him.

She's yelling. Yell louder. Someone—something, tells me. But why? When has any of my own voices told me to do that?

"Who are you to yell at us?" I scream at the teacher. I think this is another time when I've just pictured it in my mind, but she is actually looking at me. Am I standing??

"You want to get sent to detention?"

Usually, I would look down. I would take it. That's my dad's side talking. This, though, is my mom's side talking. I can't sit around and take it anymore.

As she sends me out of the room, I realize Anxiety is having a whole panic attack. As my heart races, my head gets light and the hallway becomes darker. I end up blacking out.

"Ugh…"

I hear a voice just faintly in my head. I'm not awake. Far from it, actually.

Her voice is my voice. She's my encouragement even when I can't see her, yet that isn't her name. She's confident that I can manage to keep going. She feels more supportive than my own parents. She is my calm before the next storm, but she's always there. I've never even met her, but I know all of this about her instantly.

She is the one who encourages me. She tells me I still have worth in this world, and yet she doesn't make it sound the same as when Anxiety tells that story. When she says it, I believe her. She tells me the things that I need to hear to move on: be that "life of the party" that people call me.

"When you need me, find me. Find me inside of nature, in the beat of every song you listen to, in every laugh you hear, and in every gust of wind that passes through your hair. Live like there's no tomorrow, because tomorrow is not a promise, like those two chapel leaders said."

I see her as I look from the ground up to this being. She looks like an Angel. She sits next to me and gives me a hug. Well, it really doesn't feel like a hug, but it's better.

"They said it differently," I say with a small

chuckle.

"Ehh... Don't listen to how they said it. Give me some time. Trust me. These creeps in your head that have held you back... they won't be a bother soon enough. I can help you." She giggles, and with one last embrace, her form becomes that of a small child. The beauty never fades. The feeling around her never changes. She lets me go and gives a warm smile before she skips away from me. She stops one last time to look back at me. Her face reflects me. She looks like that 5-year-old me that still had hope.

"What is it?" I ask. She smiles brighter.

"Enjoy it. There's meaning in misery. You'll see, later. You will come to understand that you would do it all again to become the girl you are now and the girl you will be later—even if they, the dark clouds hovering over you, take you through hell. It's nothing compared to what's to come," she explains, removing my ability to find words that will work for my mouth. This, from a child, is what I've needed to hear all along to keep me going.

As she fades away, I regain consciousness. I'm not sad about leaving her, because I'm really not leaving her. I wake up on a couch, three people are around me.

"She's awake." I realize the people above me are the teacher, the principal, and one of the pastors who happened to be in the area as I passed out.

I jump awake, laughing.

"Are you crazy?"

"I'm perfect. I met… My Little Angel."

Chapter 4: Step Back

"That's how you describe it…?" The woman at the desk in front of me asks. I stay seated on her couch within the therapy office.

I chuckle, "Well, yeah? My story, right?"

"You still feel that way?"

"No."

"Why are you here then…? You told me your story. How should I help you if…you don't need me?"

"Everybody has times when they need help… You just started off by asking what my experience has been like."

"Well, I'm curious… How are you now?"

How am I? That's the question I'm sure a lot of people wonder, especially after that story. Truth be told, I'm not happy yet, although I can say that even though I don't smile all the time, I smile more. Over this past summer, many things have happened, some fun, some not so great.

The problem is that I believe people don't realize that words stick. Sticks and stones do break bones, but the rest of the saying is a lie: "but words will never hurt me." Anyone who says that is kidding themselves. They might say that with full confidence around people, but they get home and have a different story wrapped around their mind. Words eat at us, especially the bad ones. Their pettiness can bring people down at random times until they think, "Am I ever going to escape this?"

I would know.

Even in recent times, more struggles reveal themselves, leaving more wounds. Every wound takes time to heal. It doesn't matter if it's a bleeding wound or mental wound, every wound takes time to heal. And with every healed wound, especially the deep wounds, there are scars. There are physical scars and there are mental scars.

Point being, even if the wound is fully healed, we will look back at it. Even with physical wounds, seeing that scar—depending on our mentality—occasionally sets off something in the brain that makes the person want to re–open their wounds. It's not healthy, but it's life. And some people are way more scarred mentally than others.

I believe we should be mindful of that before comparing traumas. I've heard people have a tendency to "one–up" each other's traumas. That kind of one–upmanship leaves more scars for me. This story is about finding peace. There is peace in the madness; it just takes longer to find for some people. That's not something to brag and be willingly prideful about.

I bet people will think that my mother's diagnosis left that kind of wound or scar for me, but no. The idea for this story came from before her prognosis of only a year to live, which came in December 2021. That was nearly two full years ago, and she is still standing with us to this day. God has granted her more time to live. It is nothing but a scratch to me now.

It took me five years to find my peace. During those years, my wounds couldn't heal because I wouldn't let them. I learned at a young age that people disappoint other people. Those scars from years ago still get opened to this day, and although it's not healthy, it's all I've ever known.

The difference is, I've learned how to take a step back. In the writing of this story, I learned to take a step back. The Angel in this story is my step back, my acceptance, and my moving forward. It's the child in me that can still do that.

Before writing this chapter, I was overwhelmed, having a panic attack, struggling. So, I went outside—using cleaning my shoes as an excuse to do so—and sat down on a swing in my backyard. I closed my eyes and realized that this struggle had a purpose. I wouldn't have been listening to the birds and the whistling winds if it weren't for these hardships. I wouldn't be in God's outdoor creation if I didn't have a storm before the peace.

Taking a step back is realizing that if we stop and take a look around, life moves on. Everything passes and time keeps ticking. It's not so fun, but if worrying takes up all the time in the day, it's going to make life pass by too fast. Rather than being held back, all it takes is letting it go and moving on with life rather than against it, living in the past.

"Life moves pretty fast. If you don't stop and take a look around once in a while, you could miss it." Ferris Bueller said that in a movie. It's a matter of not running from our problems when things get tough. It's knowing that something is going to help even when nothing else has. Those choices to look for what may help has risks, but sometimes it's all for a greater good.

And so, I say to my listeners and readers who have struggled in life: Your life has a purpose, and you are loved. People will hurt you. People will stab you in the back and call it an accident. People will take your very soul if you let them.

So, take that step back and find what's good for you. Take that risk you want to take, the one that will lead you to peace.

You will heal.

You still matter.

Scary Movies

By Kara (AK) Evans

Age 15

My Grandma Nita is the oldest daughter, but the middle child in her family. They lived in simple times. Her dad did construction and he worked seven days a week. Her mom stayed at home, so they always had dinner together (her mom was an excellent cook). It was important to them that the family stayed together. Her mom also made the majority of their clothes.

Nita loved scary movies. On nights when the movies were playing on TV, Nita and her little brother snuck downstairs after everyone was asleep and watched the movie. One night she stayed up late and watched a werewolf movie, after which she went back to bed. The clock in her room was making strange noises. One of the hands on the clock was bent, so as it went around it scratched the base. My grandma was still on edge from the movie.

"Who's there?" she called after a while. Her mom heard from downstairs and went up to investigate. Nita's mom always styled her hair to be big and poofy. When

Nita heard the scratching noises from her clock and saw her mom's hair and her eyes looking at her, she thought her mom was a werewolf. My grandma screamed bloody murder! Her mom then knew that she had been up watching scary movies again.

She got in trouble because she wasn't supposed to watch them, but that didn't stop her. She continued to watch the movies and has many other funny stories of the things that happened on those nights.

Not So Small Miracles

By Charissa Fryberger

Whether we are on the far side of the world or nestled comfortably at home, our days are full of little miracles—celestial graces that facilitate or adorn our lives and remind us that God is always present. One of the reasons that I like to travel is that when I am struggling to navigate life under unfamiliar circumstances, I notice His interventions more readily and see them more clearly for what they are: divine touches into my ordinary terrestrial existence.

My daughter, Aspen, and I had a lovely time in the Middle East—wonderful both because of the magic of traveling in unknown and unimagined places and because of the gift of spending extended time exploring with my daughter. Our adventures, both the planned and the unexpected, were better because we were together. That doesn't mean we were always of like mind. On our first day in the bustling city of Istanbul, with shopkeepers trying to engage us on all sides (which was a bit intimidating at first), Aspen declared, "I don't talk to anyone."

"Aspen, I talk to everyone," I countered. That

required the first of many compromises as we learned to adapt our styles and habits to accommodate each other. The trip, however, began with a bit of a mishap that required both of us to adjust to the common complications of international travel.

On our way to Istanbul, we were scheduled to change planes in Amsterdam with only an hour on the ground. It was a dash across the airport, but we made it; our luggage didn't. That was neither a huge nor an unusual problem—airlines deal with lost luggage every day. We filled out the paperwork, and Turkish Air promised to bring our belongings to our Airbnb the next day. Since we each had a toothbrush and spare clothes in our carryon backpacks, we weren't too fussed. We got on the bus for the 90-minute ride into the city with pretty good confidence of seeing our suitcases again.

The bus dropped us in the middle of the Old City where the GPS on Aspen's phone predicted a mile and a half hike to where we were staying. As we walked, the streets got narrower and more deserted. It was getting dark, and our surroundings looked sketchier and sketchier. The GPS coordinates (street addresses in the Middle East proved to be insufficient most of the time) combined with two pages of written directions, and the photographs our host had posted on the Airbnb site finally took us up a narrow street (an alley by any American standard), then turned us into a narrower alley where we found an industrial metal door with a keypad lock. Inside was a courtyard that doubled as extra seating for a little restaurant in the early mornings and as a salvage yard the rest of the day. We crossed to the back of the courtyard to find another door with a keypad lock.

Inside we were met by the Airbnb host who took us up a very narrow winding staircase to the third floor and unlocked our room. It was small, but big enough, and it had a hotplate and little fridge so Aspen could cook once we re-acquired our luggage containing her frying pan (because of her food allergies, she can rarely eat in restaurants).

The host tried to explain the particulars of the place to us in Turkish, but we weren't communicating well. Finally, he decided to try writing something down to help us understand and asked me to hand him the pen on the table. It turns out that the word for pen in Turkish is the same as in Russian. My ear heard the familiar word and, without thinking, I responded in Russian. I realized what I had done and felt a little silly. I started to apologize, but the man interrupted, "Oh, Russian. Da." We switched to Russian and did just fine. It surprised both Aspen and I; I hadn't expected my Russian to be valuable in Turkey.

After he left, we realized that the airline would

never find us in this side alley behind three locked doors. We tried to call, but couldn't get past the phone tree, so we hoped they would call us when they found they couldn't deliver. We hung around the next morning, but never heard from them. The following day, we got up early and retraced our path to the airport where we were passed from person to person to person (seven in all, I think) before our cause was taken up by a very young attendant who seemed to know where our luggage was. He was a cheerful fellow who sang to himself as he led us around twists and turns through the bowels of the Istanbul Airport to where he finally reunited us with our bags--and Aspen's frying pan. Success!

That was the first miracle of the day, but a second was coming.

That afternoon, after about six miles of oohing and ahhhing over the sights of Istanbul, Aspen and I sat down to rest on a stone wall in the corner of a courtyard between two of the city's most famous mosques. It was filled with tourists. When I say "filled" I mean it looked like a street festival in Denver. We discussed where to go next and then headed down the street toward the Golden Horn (the horn-shaped harbor that enriched Istanbul with maritime trade throughout the Greek, Roman, Byzantines, and Ottoman eras). About a mile later, I stopped to use a WC (public restroom) and realized that I didn't have my cell phone. Immediately, we reversed our steps and headed back for the crowded courtyard. As we climbed the hill, I prayed for a Good Samaritan to find my phone, and for us to somehow find him.

On returning to our resting place, we (not surprisingly) found no phone. However, an officer in a police tent across the way noticed us searching and asked (in English!) if we were looking for a phone. When I described it, he showed me a picture on his phone that displayed all the contents of my phone case: Colorado driver's license, Visa card, 110 Lira (Turkish currency) and a $20 bill (US). He then led us across the park and in the back way to the police station, where we met three officers sitting at a table under a tree trying to jailbreak my phone with a paperclip so that they could find my contact information. I think they were almost as excited to find me and return the phone to me as I was relieved to receive it back. God truly had provided very official-looking Good Samaritans. They were all amazed that among the thousands of tourists there, we had managed to find each other so they could return the phone to the right person. One of them pointed up and said it could only have been God. I couldn't have agreed more.

And so, thanks to God's miraculous touch and several kind and conscientious Turkish policemen, we continued our trip without the disaster of canceling phones and credit cards and then doing without them in a foreign country. I also have, among my stories of visiting Istanbul, an experience that is recommended in none of the tourist literature: filling out a Turkish police report.

What can I say but, "Thanks be to God!"

FICTION

Journeys of Korfire

By Kara (AK) Evans

Age 15

Chapter one: Meet the Captain

The deep blue waters spring up in a salty mist. The smell of sea air and, quite frankly, fish whips through the cold night. Very few clouds cover the sky. This is perfect because it does not hinder the beauty and majesty of the starry night. Blue and purple swirl amongst the blackness that encircles the constellation of the great water dragon, Dylan, above. On nights like this one, I can almost see him shining down on any and all sailors who happen to be out this late at night.

I am hanging off the mast of my ship, the *Starlight Crusader*, looking up at Dylan. "Why can't I find you?" I whisper into the night air. I know that Dylan is real. I know because the stories about his son, Wavan, are true. I know this because when I was sixteen years old, I received the ability to control the wind from him. This ability to control the wind is what the Legends say will happen once in every generation. Over the years, I have come to the conclusion that all the old stories and legends about the gods are true. "Dylan, where are you?" The air whips my long, braided hair back from my face.

"Captain, I need you down here," the voice of my first mate, Stellamaris, drifts up to my ears from the deck where she is constantly working to keep the ship running. (I have never acquired any more crew. Why should I? Stellamaris and I can function perfectly fine without others complicating the picture). Jumping to a rope, I twist, turn, and flip all the way to the deck of the *Starlight Crusader*.

"What's going on Stellamaris?"

"There seems to be some sort of disturbance in the water up ahead, Captain."

"What do you think it is?" I ask.

"I'm not sure. However, I do think it may be wise to turn the ship around."

"Ok, I trust you."

As I am preparing to climb back up the mast to use the power of Wavan to turn the ship into the natural flow of the wind, all of a sudden, my eyes catch sight of another ship, this one bright red and bearing the symbol of Alroth upon the flag. It is skipping over the waves coming straight for us.

"Stellamaris, prepare for company," I call down to the deck, pushing my hands out in front of my body, and straining with all my might so that I am quickly able to change the wind to my favour. In doing so, I turn the *Starlight Crusader* away from the strange current in the water.

After a while, the red ship bearing the sign of Alroth is gaining on us. *The captain of that ship is very smart, manoeuvring his or her ship into the slipstream of mine so as not to have to fight the wind that would normally be pushing against them,* I think. "There's only one pirate as smart as that who still sails the sea," I murmur, looking down to the deck of the approaching ship. "Orion." Sure enough, as I say the word, I spot him standing on the bridge, looking straight up at me from the wheel of his ship. Swinging back to the deck, I anxiously prepare for Orion's arrival.

"Who is coming? Who sails that ship, Captain?"

"An old friend," I answer simply. "Stellamaris, grab some rum from below deck, please." Though I am the captain and am not required to say 'please,' Stellamaris is more than a first mate; she is my friend, and I trust her.

"Aye aye, Captain," Stellamaris says and leaves without any other questions. Moments later, Orion's ship pulls alongside the *Starlight Crusader*.

"Permission to board, Captain?"

"Permission granted, my friend," I reply, looking into the face of Orion standing straight and tall at the edge of the railing. I grab a board that lies next to the rail and place it between the two ships, creating a bridge for Orion to walk across. Orion quickly and nimbly leaps onto the board. In three strides, he has crossed to the deck of the *Starlight Crusader*.

"Orion! It is so good to see you!" A smile breaks through the stern expression that is usually plastered to my face. I open my arms and we embrace.

"Korfire! It has been a very long time."

"Korfire? I have not heard my name spoken in so long. It is a strange and pleasant sensation," I say thoughtfully.

"Really? What then does your first mate call you?" Orion asks, looking into my face with a strange expression. His dark eyebrows are knitted together as a slight frown crosses his lips.

"She simply refers to me as Captain. It simplifies matters," I respond, shrugging my shoulders to indicate that I don't really care.

"Does she even know your name?" Orion asks.

"No," I respond. Orion looks almost shocked by this. I'm not entirely sure why. After all, he has known me for almost thirty-five years now. Orion and I are Elves so we live far longer than regular humans (though I still look about 20). Orion, of all the people in the world, knows how I operate. "Please do not mention my name to Stellamaris. You know as well as I that there are many powerful people who'd give almost anything to see me dead. I have not told Stellamaris my name to protect her."

"Korfire, I will not tell her. In all honesty, I am shocked, but not entirely surprised, given your history, that you have not told, uhh… Stellamaris, is it?"

"Yes. She was named for the brightest star in the sky."

"So, how about some food?" Orion says changing the topic to food as is his usual fashion.

"Yes. Stellamaris should have gotten the rum by now." Sure enough, as I turn, I see Stellamaris climbing the stairs with three bottles of rum under her arm.

"I have the rum, Captain," she says. "Shall I take it to your cabin?"

"Yes, that is a splendid idea," I say, quick and sure of my words now.

"Shall I simply leave the bottles on the table for your friend and yourself? Then I will leave the two of you alone if that be your wish ma'am."

"No, Stellamaris. You may stay and sit with us if you like."

64

"Aye, Captain. I think I shall stay with you as long as you allow it."

"Then let us not stand around talking anymore. Let us discuss all things that need discussing over a meal and rum," Orion says, putting an arm around my shoulders and walking with me toward my cabin.

A small table in the corner of my quarters is covered in maps, papers, and books. Candle wax has melted on one corner of the table from long nights of reading and planning. I stride over to the table and start rolling up my maps and papers. Stellamaris jumps in and begins putting books back onto the shelves that line the walls. These shelves are filled with books, maps, pictures, rocks, teeth of sea creatures, daggers and even my swords. The swords are some of my favourites. There is a wide variety of them: Normal, Enchanted, Broadswords, Cutlasses, Scimitars, Cavalry Sabers, and Rapiers. Each has a use and a purpose. Each has a story to tell, and every single one is sharpened to perfection. All are deadly weapons when wielded by my skillful hand.

After the table has been cleared and the candle wax scraped from the corner, we all take our seats. Stellamaris speaks first as per usual.

"So, Orion, why have you travelled so far to see the captain?" Stellamaris says suspiciously.

"I have simply come to visit an old friend. Is that a problem?"

"No, it is not, except for the fact that many do not simply sail the seas to find an old friend unless it is, in fact, very important." Stellamaris looks deep into Orion's eyes. I know what she is doing. She has, over the years, learned to understand complex body language. Just by looking at someone, she can not only tell when they are lying, but know what they are lying about. She can sometimes even guess what they are thinking before the person even speaks.

"I see you have taught your first mate well, Captain," Orion says, looking at me. As promised, as long as Stellamaris is in the room, he will not address me by my true name. I smile and turn to Stellamaris.

"Stella, you have done well, but we may find the answers we seek if only we let the poor man speak," I say kindly but firmly to inform her that I am well aware of the situation and will handle it.

"Yes ma'am," Stellamaris responds and sitsback in her seat slightly, letting Orion have the stage.

Chapter Two: Old Friends and Strange Beginnings

"Alright, Orion, let's have it. Why are you here? By no means is this an unpleasant surprise, but I do want to know what you have that needs to be discussed?"

"Well, Captain, I have had suspicions about what you are up to for quite a long time. I need to be sure what you are doing, and, if it is what I suspect, I want to join you, my friend."

"What is it you think I am doing?" I ask, slightly concerned that he does indeed know that I am searching for Dylan.

"Captain, do not act as if you think I am stupid. We have known each other since we were ten years old. You, my friend, are searching for…" Orion stops short when his first mate begins pounding on the cabin door.

"Captain Orion! We have a big problem up here!" Both Orion and I stand up immediately. Stellamaris is only a step behind us. *Why has Orion's first mate come to sound an alarm?*

"What is going on?" Orion asks as he bursts out of my cabin and onto the deck of the *Starlight Crusader*. However, I, being the captain of the ship, do not stop to ask questions. Instead, I sprint for the mast. Jumping nimbly up, I scale the mast in under a minute. Looking out, I can see a ship moving towards us.

"Captain!" I hear Orion's voice calling to me from below. I look down to see a spyglass in his crewmate's hands. Sometimes I forget that other people do not have as keen of eyesight as Orion and I, for Elves, of all the creatures in Madulellein, have the ability to see three times farther than the most farsighted humans.

"What?" I call back to Orion.

"The ship…"

"I know I can see it!"

"The ship belongs to A-wut!" Orion's voice is

strange now, although I seem to be the only one who hears the strain in his voice.

No, not just strain. I think *There is also fear and shock.* I am shocked as well. *A-wut? How?* I thought that he was dead. No, I was sure that he died. If indeed he is alive, how did he manage to find us?

"Are you sure it is his?" I call to Orion.

"Yes. Look to the nest of the ship. There!" He points as he says it. "You can see him. It is A-wut, no doubt." I see him now. He is sneering across at me.

"Stellamaris, I need you up here!" I yell down to her. A moment later she stands next to me on the mast spar, prepared to do anything I request.

"Stellamaris, I need you to hide my maps, my journals, and…" I pause. *Is this too much to ask of her?* I give my head a quick shake and continue. "I need you to move the chest."

"The chest?!" Her eyes open wide with shock.

"Yes. That is what he wants. He has wanted it since long before you were even born."

"Why?"

"The why is not important right now. I just need to know if you are up to the task of hiding it."

"I am," Stellamaris replies and climbs quickly back down to the deck. I see her dismount and run towards my cabin, brushing off all the questions Orion asks.

I take one more look at the fast-approaching ship then jump to a nearby rope and slide back to where Orion stands.

"Korfire," he says quietly as he walks toward me. "What are we going to do?"

"I don't know. Ah! This is exactly why I have not yet told Stellamaris my name. I didn't want someone like A-wut hurting her or finding us," I say smacking my forehead in frustration.

"How is A-wut even still alive?" Orion asks me.

"I don't know. Unless…" I trail off thinking hard. *There was only one other person there on that fateful day—only one explanation as to how he could be here twenty five years after he 'died.'* I look to Orion and see that he has followed my train of thought.

"Maldu," Orion says, a grim expression set hard on his face.

"Maldu always was a clever one. Though I can't believe he actually went back to save A-wut after everything Maldu went through at A-wut's hands."

"I can't believe it either. Unless…"

"Unless he had no choice?"

"Exactly. I mean A-wut knew how to enslave people's wills with magic. If A-wut didn't want to lose his servant, I have no doubt that he could take Maldu's will without giving a second thought to whether it was too cruel."

"That makes sense."

"Korfire, can you face him again?" Orion asks suddenly, grabbing my hand and staring into my eyes. His face is serious with a faint tinge of concern on it. I bristle. *I know why you are asking. I will face him over and over again, as long as it takes for me to be free of him.* Though the thought is not a pleasant one, I know that it is true.

"Yes. I don't know why you are asking," I say shrugging my shoulders to hide the shudders that shoot up my spine.

"Korfire, you're afraid, aren't you?"

"Why do you say that?" *Dang Napit! He's looking at my eyes.* Very few people know my secret, and Orion is one of those few people.

"Korfire, your eyes have turned purple. We both know full well what that means." He's right. Usually, my eyes are Sea green rimmed with a dark teal and blue. When I get angry or fired up, my eyes become orange and yellow encircled by fiery red; but when I am scared, my eyes will turn violet and deep purple. "Korfire, it's okay to be scared. I might be more worried if you weren't."

"It isn't okay to be scared," I say, trying to stand a little taller.

"Yes, it is. Korfire, you're not just facing some villain of the seas…"

"Don't say it, Orion!" I say, cutting him off and

looking around to make sure nobody is eavesdropping. He continues anyway.

"You're facing your father." With these words dread drops into my stomach.

My father.

Chapter 3: Family Matters

Chills run down my spine. I never in a million years could have guessed that fate should be so cruel as to force me to face him again.

"He's not my father," I say, trying to stand even taller so as to look unafraid. Orion simply looks at me. I know that he can see through my facade, but I cannot fall to pieces while Orion's crew looks on. Any sign of weakness could mean lack of obedience when the battle inevitably arrives, and disobedience in such a crucial time could end in death. Orion knows this, so he remains silent.

Just as it looks like Orion will open his mouth to say something else (though quietly), Stellamaris ascends the steps from my cabin.

"Oh, good she's back," Orion says instead of what he was obviously planning to say to me. "If somebody were to tell me what you two are planning, I could help you." He looks back and forth between us.

"Stellamaris was hiding the chest," I say, not mentioning the removal of all my documents as well.

"Yes, and you will be pleased to know that it is nearly impossible to find without a detailed knowledge of this specific ship and all the alterations made to it," she informed me.

"Good work. Jaklone linado Stella hino washlade." I say the last part in Maldomic. In the common tongue it translates into, "Thank you Stella my friend."

"Linado tae minlano, hino Braque (You are welcome, my Captain)," she says, nodding her head in respect.

"Captain, you do realize that if he was able to find you, he most likely has the plans to your ship," Orion says. He, too, can speak the language of Maldomic. Being able to speak Maldomic has many upsides. For one, our conversations can be held in secret even in public. Two, Maldomic is much more meaningful than the common tongue. For instance, if you want to say, 'I love you' in the common tongue that is simply what you would say. In Maldomic, love has different words with different meanings. 'Karlotith' is the general term for love but 'Larb' is a deep and personal love.

"Yes, Orion, I know. That is why I have made the alterations with only the help of Stellamaris. She and I are the only ones who know the absolute layout of the ship."

"Captain, may I ask again, why is this A-wut chasing after you? And why is the chest important?" Stella asks.

"Keep your voice down Stella. If you are to speak of the chest say, 'Maldopt' for few people speak Maldomic anymore. To answer your questions is to explain a story for which we have neither the time nor I the heart to tell you yet," I say, looking sadly at Stellamaris, who will have to wait a while longer to understand the gravity of this situation. I do need her to know one thing, however. "Stella, because you have hidden the Maldopt, if A-wut finds out he will torture you. I know that I can trust you, and you know that I will not let him harm you. If I tell you to hide you must do so."

"Yes, Captain," she says nodding her head.

"No matter what, Stella, you must hide if he finds out that you are the one who has hidden the Maldopt." I grab her shoulders to make sure she understands the gravity of what I am telling her.

"I understand," she says.

"Kor… Captain," Orion says changing at top speed to avoid speaking my real name. Stellamaris is looking at him in confusion. She caught his mistake but doesn't know what kind of mistake was made.

"What is it?" I ask.

"The sea is moving strangely behind us, "Orion responds.

"What?!"

"He's right, Captain. Look behind you!" Stella says, shock in her eyes.

I turn around to see that Orion and Stellamaris are right. A giant whirlpool has formed directly behind us; but it is not a normal whirlpool like some I have seen on occasion over the years. It is moving in almost a triangle shape, not a circle. The water is bashing against itself, spraying the *Starlight Crusader* with drops.

"Shalshat zastaria aget farlassa! (By the stars and sea!)" I exclaim. I know in my heart what is down there, but my mind does not believe it.

"Braque! (Captain!)" Orion shouts. I turn back to see his expression clouded with fear. He is pointing toward A-wut's ship, now too close for any comfort. "In coming!" There, sailing on the wind as if it has wings: a cannonball.

"Take cover!" I scream as it comes closer. The entirety of Orion's crew jumps over barrels and crates of food to find some sort of cover. Only Orion, Stella, and I are still standing when the cannonball hits. The impact sends the ship rocking violently. Orion and Stella manage to hang on, but I am thrown overboard. As I fall into the water, my head smacks against the side of the ship. *I am going to die.* This is my last thought as I sink down into the dark water, bubbles floating around me. I can faintly hear Orion screaming my name before everything goes as black as the sky above.

* * *

Coughing. Water exiting my lungs violently onto the deck. These are the first things I am aware of. *Where am I? What happened…Why am I not dead?* My head is pounding, and I feel weak. I try to open my eyes.

"Ow"

Wow, that was pitiful. I don't even know who is beyond the blackness of my closed eyes, and my first words are 'Ow?' I could be in serious danger right now, and all I can say is 'Ow?' Great job, Korfire.

"Father, I mean Captain, she's stirring." That voice. I have heard that voice before. *Maldu.* That means that I am not on the *Starlight Crusader* or even Orion's ship *Alroth's Revenge* as I hoped I'd be. There is only one place that I can be if I am hearing Maldu's voice. *My father's ship. This is not good!*

"Ah, very good. Take her down to my cabin before she fully wakes up and causes difficulties." That voice sends a cold shiver of fear down my spine. I struggle once again to open my eyes. My head is pounding. I groan softly.

"Korfire, don't worry. You're safe now," Maldu whispers softly and kindly in my ear. *Oh yeah, right. Safe. Totally safe. Definitely not like I'm on my evil father's ship. My father who really wants me dead. Yeah, I'm totally safe.* I think sarcastically.

I'm still not having the easiest time breathing after my plunge into the icy waters and swallowing half the ocean. My lungs feel like they are on fire, but I try to speak anyway.

"Why?" I manage to get out before I start coughing, and my lungs turn to a blazing inferno inside of me.

"He's changed, Korfire. He really has this time!" Maldu says excitedly. The light that had been coming through the lids of my closed eyes suddenly disappears. *I must be inside of A-wut's cabin now,* I think. Maldu sets me down on something soft. This time when I try to open my eyes, I manage it. I can see Maldu standing next to me, joy on his face.

"Minlano akluck chung (Welcome back my little sister)."

Chapter 4: Dylan

"Don't call me that!" I say as harshly as possible while still trying to recover from sea water. "You are no longer my brother! Not after you helped him!"

"Sister, when I helped him the first time, I had no choice. Our father had me under the curse of dark magic! Now I am helping him because he has changed."

"Yeah, I call attacking my friends and I pretty changed." The sarcasm rolling from my tongue like plumes of fire!

"He wasn't firing at you! He was firing at the water behind you, but he miscalculated!"

"Why in Dylan's name should A-wut care about

hitting the water?" I ask, exasperated by my brother's blindness.

"Because, sister, you are much closer to finding the thing you seek than you realize," Maldu says with relish in his voice. I can tell that he wants to say more, but just then A-wut steps down the stairs. I try to sit up to take a defensive position. Maldu pushes me back down. "Blonk plong (Lay still)," Maldu commands gently.

"Korfire, my daughter, how I have missed you these past twenty years," A-wut says in a deep and ragged voice. His voice is still gravely but some part of it is softer, kinder almost. *I still don't trust you, no matter how nice you sound. You tried to kill me and all of the people I care about. I will never forget what you have done,* I tell him silently. I give him a glare that tells him exactly what I was just thinking.

"Darling please…"

"No! You don't get to call me that! You lost your right to call me 'darling,' 'daughter,' 'sweetheart'—any of those things! You lost those rights when you tried to KILL me! When you tried to destroy my WHOLE WORLD!" I scream at him, my voice cracking on the words 'whole world.' Who is my whole world? That is the one who has always been there for me, and the one I have always and will always love. *Orion.*

"Korfire, that was twenty years ago. I admit that I have done some pretty terrible things, but I am a changed elf now."

"Sister, he is telling the truth. Why do you think that he pulled you out of the water?"

"To use me as leverage the same way he did last time," I say hotly.

"Korfire…" Maldu starts, with a pleading tone. I know that it is his desire for us to be a family again. A normal family. *Well, as normal as it can get when you're a pirate family.* I can't fulfil his wish, however. I can never trust my father again.

"No." I force the word out in the most law-setting voice I can manage. I push myself up and swing my legs over the side of A-wut's cot. A-wut takes a step toward me, probably to make me lie down again. I throw my left hand up defensively and, with the right, reach for the sword that I always have strapped to my hip. My hand closes on empty air. "Where is my sword?" I snarl at my father.

"You didn't think we would allow you to keep weapons while you are aboard, did you? We don't know how bitter you still are. And I am glad. Otherwise, I must defend myself from you," A-wut says, smiling smugly.

"Did I ask you why? No! I asked where my sword *is*," I respond scathingly.

"It is on the deck, but you shall not have it… yet," A-wut answers. *So what if he doesn't give it back to me? I can take it back,* I tell myself. I can tell that my father and Maldu have not stripped me of all my weapons. I can feel three of my daggers strapped under my shirt, I can also feel my disguised pistol concealed at my hip. Most importantly of all, they have not taken my ring from me. *Wait, is he looking at my eyes right now?*

"Korfire, are your eyes turning red?" A-wut asks. *Dang Napit. He knows.* I'd forgotten he was one who knew.

I am preparing to spring forward to begin my attack when a sudden lurch of the ship sends all three of us flying across the cabin. A-wut and Maldu are lying six feet from me. I look up and realize that the door is only three feet from where I have landed. *I can make it!* It takes only a second for me to get to my feet and another two to reach the door and fling it open. I climb the stairs to the deck before either my father or brother can get to their feet. When I reach the deck, A-wut's crew is sprawled across the entire deck.

"Shalshat zastaria aget farlassa! (By the stars and sea!) What in the name of Dylan happened here?!" I'm shocked.

"Korfire!" I hear A-wut's voice coming closer. *Get a move on Korfire,* I tell myself sternly. I see my sword hanging at the hip of one of the crew members. I rush over, snatching it from his belt, and sprint for the helm. The moment I reach the helm, I can see that the strange whirlpool from before has somehow moved around the *Starlight Crusader* and is now almost upon my father's ship.

"This is not possible!" I exclaim. "No natural

thing of the sea can move like that. Not unless, but it can't be…" I trail off trying to think of some explanation for this phenomenon.

"Sister, we have to get out of here!" Maldu calls to me from the deck below.

"I'm not going anywhere with you!"

"Korfire, be reasonable!" A-wut says. As I open my mouth to yell back a loud deep gurgling begins to emanate from inside the whirlpool. I hear a voice inside of my head.

"Korfire, Daughter of the Ocean and Skies. You have been searching for years to find the god of the ocean. You have not known why you searched but simply that you must. Korfire, you have searched because I have told you to search. I am the one who has guided you to this place. I am he for whom you search."

"Dylan!" I whisper, dropping down to one knee in reverence. "Why has the god of the sea called me and no one else?" I ask.

"You are the one about whom it was foretold thousands of years ago that you would become the champion of the gods and vanquish evil from every corner of ocean, land, and sky. You will be honoured above all others. Korfire you shall be the victor for all the world."

"M-me? How can I be the champion of the gods? I am a pirate."

"Your heart is right for the task set before you."

"If the gods wish it, I will do it," I say though my heart is sinking at the thought of being 'Champion' and having to give up my life of adventure.

"You misunderstand me. You will not have to live in a palace or be commander of an army. No. No, your task will be to search the world for any pieces of ancient relics that cause a disturbance in the course of mortal events. This task will be dangerous, and you will have to sacrifice many things along the way; but this means you will not only be the champion of the gods, but also the greatest pirate ever known to sail the nine seas." Dylan pauses for a moment. My mind is racing. *Am I going to have to do this alone?* Dylan seemed to sense my thoughts.

"You will need help. Though not many people may know your true task, Orion, and Stellamaris will travel with you. These are the only two whom you may tell of your quest. Go now, Korfire, Captain of the *Starlight Crusader*, Champion of the gods. Bring peace to the mortal world. In order to accomplish this task, you must first forgive your father. You do not have to *like* him, but for your heart to be whole, you must learn to forgive."

"Okay, I forgive him," I say, and suddenly I feel a weight lift off of my chest, something I never realized I had been carrying for so many years.

"Now you are ready. Now I must go…"

"Wait, can I at least see you?" I ask, hesitation in my voice. I know that it is silly, but I really want to see what he looks like. Could Dylan be anything like how I imagined him? In answer, an enormous dragon with all the shades of the ocean tides woven together throughout his scales and a head the size of the *Starlight Crusader* appears roaring out of the water. Dylan has something like whiskers coming off of his face, but they look eerily similar to seaweed. *Dylan can fly!* I realize, watching him rise. I can hear screaming coming from behind me, but I don't care. Dylan circles around me once in the air, sprinkling water all over and around me. All of the sudden, I feel as if I am the water flowing and moving with the ocean. Next thing I know, I am waking up on *my* bed blinking up at the ceiling in *my* cabin on *my* ship.

"What happened?" I'm whispering, but I don't know why I bother.

"Korfire? Are you awake?" I hear Orion's voice ask quietly. I turn to see him sitting next to me and realize that my hands are clasped tightly in his.

"Orion, what happened? How did I get back here?" I ask again.

"I don't really understand how. When the cannon ball hit, you went over the side. I jumped in after you, but A-wut got there first. He took you aboard his ship. You were there for at least thirty minutes before some sort of blue and green mist began rising out of the whirlpool. When the mist passed over A-wut's ship, his entire crew just collapsed where they were. Then Stellamaris and I watched as you knelt on the helm of A-wut's ship and looked into the whirlpool. You didn't stay there for more than ten minutes, but then something exploded out of the water. After that you were hurled by the rocking of A-wut's ship back into the water. I jumped back into the water to pull you out, but you were already on the deck of this ship. Stellamaris and I carried you in here. You've been out for three hours now."

"Orion, it was Dylan who exploded out of the water as you say. Dylan was the one in the whirlpool. Dylan was the one I talked to. Dylan is real." I can feel myself smiling.

"You're smiling again. That makes twice in one day; that is rare. You better get a hold on yourself, Korfire. You don't want people to think you're going soft, now do you?" Orion says grinning back at me.

"I can't help it. First, I see you again for the first time in years, and then I talk to Dylan and he tells me--he tells me…" I stumble remembering what Dylan had said.

"What did he tell you?"

"He told me that I am the Champion of the gods, the one who was foretold thousands of years ago. He also said that you and Stella are to travel with me."

"Are you playing with me?"

"No, that is what Dylan told me."

"Why did he want Stellamaris and me?"

"Because you are the ones I can trust the most."

"That explains why *you* want us, but why does *Dylan* want us?"

"Because if I trust you then Dylan can trust you. So obviously *you* are the ones who are supposed to come with me. Please Orion, I don't just want you I *need* you!"

"Well then, we better tell Stellamaris and begin whatever task the Champion is to complete," Orion says, still smiling.

"Where is Stella?"

"Sailing the ship away from your father. She said 'One of us has to steer the ship, and I will not allow some strange captain to run *my* captain's ship, even if they are supposed best friends. Besides, someone has to look after her--the Captain that is.' So, here I am getting the scariest job ever; making sure you don't try to die on us." He gives me a wry smile.

I realize that I have to tell him how much he means to me. I mean, what if I had gotten captured and not made it back. He'd have gone on never knowing how I really feel. *Come on Korfire, just tell him,* I chide myself.

"Orion, I love you." Orion just looks at me.

"I love you too," he says in response. I know he didn't catch what I meant.

"No. No, Orion I larb you (love, a deep love)," I say, watching his face to see if he understands. "I love

you, have always loved you, and will always love you,"
I finish.

"Well then, we have something else in common,"
Orion says, squeezing my hands and giving me a quick
kiss before helping me up. We leave the cabin to find
Stellamaris and set off on our next adventure. The whole
time he never lets go of my hand, and I don't let go of
his."

The Interview

By Andrea Wade

I sat down at the table in the old coffee shop feeling nervous about this interview. Questions flew around in my continued reverie to the point that I failed to notice my contact had arrived. The sound of the chair scraping the floor across from me whipped me back into the present. I made no introduction, and without looking at Him, began the interview.

"I'd like to ask you some questions about some things I have heard and read," I began. "Questions about the validity of the information being pumped out to the masses."

He did not answer, so I continued after a second or two.

"If I am so blessed, why does it always feel like the world is crashing around me?"

He didn't answer but waited. Maybe that one was too difficult to start with. I decide to ask a few different questions.

"If I am blessed, why do I feel so numb?"

"If I am blessed, why don't I feel peace?"

Still, He didn't answer. I could feel frustration gnawing at the edges of my self-control. Perhaps He was thinking about His answers, trying to come up with a clever way to justify the hurt and sorrow spreading through this dim world.

"If I am blessed, why am I living paycheck to paycheck?"

"If I am blessed, why am I not getting promoted at work?"

"If I am blessed, why am I so worried about the future?"

He remained quiet. Did He even care? Was He going to answer any of my questions? Feeling like I was fighting a losing battle, I hit him with several questions quickly.

"If I am so blessed, why am I constantly battling depression?"

"If I am blessed, why can't I hear God?"

"If I am blessed, why do I feel so lonely?"

"If I am blessed, why do I keep falling back into bad habits?"

"If I am blessed, why did my marriage end?"

I could feel salty tears trickling down my cheeks. Frustrated that I would be so silly as to cry when I was so upset, I roughly brushed them away. I could feel my heart battling to slow down. I breathed in deep and looked at my contact for the first time.

"If I am so blessed, why don't I feel like it?"

My shoulders began to shake under the oppression of my sorrow and hurt. I dropped my eyes from His and covered my face to weep, each tear filled with anxiety, anger, and fear.

Listening to my questions with quiet understanding, He leaned forward and placed His hands on mine, gently pulling them away from my face. He handed me a napkin and began to answer.

Dear Child, the world is not falling because greater is He that is in you than he that is in the world. You are blessed."

I wiped my eyes with the napkin and blew my nose as He spoke.

"Do not be anxious about anything, but in everything by prayer and thanksgiving let your requests be made known to God. And the peace of God, which surpasses all understanding, will guard your hearts and minds in Me. You are blessed."

I breathed in deeply, listening to each word He said and realizing He was answering every question I had asked.

"You have a job and enough each day. I provide for the sparrows and clothe the flowers. How much more will I do for you? You are blessed."

"Those who wait for the Lord shall renew their strength; they shall mount up with wings like eagles; they shall run and not be weary; they shall walk and not faint. You are blessed."

"Dear one, live for today. Let the worries of tomorrow take care of themselves. You are blessed."

Feeling the anger and fear subside in me, I looked into His face and saw He was smiling at me. Why would He be smiling? Was He not taking this seriously?

"I am a refuge for the oppressed, a stronghold in times of trouble. Those who know My name will trust in Me, for I have never forsaken those who seek Me. You are blessed."

"Whoever is of God hears the words of God. The reason why you do not hear them is that you are not of God. Still, you are blessed."

"Come to me, all you who are weary and burdened, and I will give you rest. Take my yoke upon you and learn from me, for I am gentle and humble in heart, and you will find rest for your souls. For my yoke is easy and my burden is light. You are blessed."

"Return to me; I will cure you of backsliding. Yes, come to me, for I am the Lord your God. You are blessed."

"Forgiveness of all sins is available through faith in Me. You are blessed."

Feeling a warm and comforting peace spread through me, I felt tears once again fall down my face. He was talking to me, about me. I could feel His love radiating to me, despite all that I had done and the mistakes I had made. He forgave me without me holding on to my faith, without me believing He could ever take me back. He was there for me!

"As for your last question, I ask you: If

a man has a hundred sheep and one of them gets lost, will He not leave the ninety-nine on the mountain and go in search of the one that is lost? Dear one, I have come for you, my precious child. You are blessed."

Looking into His loving face, I was flooded with peace. I realized I had been looking at everything all wrong. I had been looking through the lens of the world rather than the lens of truth. Knowing I was beginning to understand, He chuckled quietly and gripped my hands tighter.

Just then the waitress came by and set coffee in front of each of us. Without looking at it I took a sip. It was my favorite order made perfectly. Then I remembered I had not ordered anything before sitting down because I was determined to get my answers. I looked to Him, the great I AM, and knew, even in this small task, He took care of me.

Notes:

> 1 John 4:4
> Philippians 4:6-7
> Matthew 6:26-30
> Isaiah 40:31
> Matthew 6:34
> Psalm 9:9
> John 8:47
> Matthew 11: 28-30
> Jeremiah 3:22
> 1 John 1:9
> Matthew 8:12

The Undead Awakening

By Giovanni Rivas

Age 13

As World War II raged on, an unprecedented and unimaginable event took place. The British Prime Minister, Winston Churchill, the Soviet General Secretary, Joseph Stalin, and American President, Franklin D. Roosevelt, along with renowned scientist, Robert Oppenheimer, found themselves in a situation that none of them could have predicted.

Amidst the chaos of war, Oppenheimer was conducting a series of mysterious experiments in a secret laboratory hidden deep underground. One fateful night, a catastrophic error occurred, leading to the accidental release of nuclear radiation capable of causing biological mutations. Unbeknownst to Roosevelt, Oppenheimer, Churchill, and Stalin, this nuclear element had the power to mutate and reanimate the living and dead.

As the night unfolded, the laboratory became ground zero for an outbreak of a new kind of zombie plague. The affected lab staff mutated into ravenous, undead creatures, thirsting for human flesh. Sensing the impending danger, Oppenheimer quickly realized that their only chance of survival was to set aside their political differences and work together. Churchill, Stalin, and Roosevelt now had to fight for their survival against waves of zombies…together.

Soon, however, there were too many zombies. In retreat, they had to leave Oppenheimer behind and flee into the secured command center of the laboratory. As he was crying for help, Oppenheimer was surrounded by ferocious zombies biting him limb from limb. In his final moments, his last words were always remembered by the group, "Remember, hope is never lost."

The group faced numersous challenges, from hordes of zombies to dwindling supplies. Surprisingly, they discovered qualities within themselves that they never knew they possessed: courage, sacrifice, and camaraderie.

As they ventured deeper into the unexplored chambers of the secret laboratory, they stumbled upon

Oppenheimer's groundbreaking research. It appeared that he had been searching for a way to reverse the effects of the radiation and restore humanity. Together, they made it their mission to carry on Oppenheimer's work and find a solution. They fought wave after wave of zombies, each battle bringing them closer to unlocking the secrets of the nuclear mutation and finding a cure.

Finally, after countless battles and sacrifices, the group managed to isolate an antidote. With great anticipation and trepidation, they administered the cure to the mutated. Miraculously, it worked! The mutated individuals transformed back into their human selves and saved the entire world.

In the end, Churchill, Stalin, and Roosevelt, forged an unexpected alliance that transcended politics and ideology. They would forever share a bond formed in a crucible of a mutated laboratory. And so, amidst all the chaos of World War II, they stood as the unlikely heroes who put aside their differences to save humanity from the clutches of the undead.

No Blood Shed

By Paul Figueroa
Age 13

A massive fire erupted as the shell of a 90mm slammed into the side of an allied bunker. Havoc was spreading as the Nazi tanks attacked from behind allied lines. Chaos was everywhere as crews scrambled to get into their armored vehicles to stop the German machinery. As all the soldiers ran out of the inflamed fortification, John ran back in, in an attempt to save the injured.

"AHHHH!" John screamed as the fortification structure gave out and collapsed on him.

*****

"Where am I?" John asked as he struggled to get up from bed. A medic ran into the tent along with several others to operate on a severely injured soldier. John got up and tapped one of the medics on the back. "Uh, hey, do you know where I am?" he asked.

"We're in the outpost. Your injuries have healed, so you're good to go," the medic said. John walked outside the tent and a jeep pulled up.

"Where to?" the driver asked.

"To the base," John ordered.

John stepped out of the jeep and walked over to his commander. "It's good to see you're doing better," the commander said.

"Where are we supposed to be?" asked John.

"We're getting ready to discuss our plan to invade the beaches of Normandy by water. Meet at the command tent in 25 minutes."

John walked into the meeting and sat down by his friend, Brody. "What is this meeting about?" he asked.

"I'm not sure," Brody said.

The commander walked into the room with a projector. He yelled, "You

might be wondering why you're here now. We are planning to attack the Germans from the water. We will send battleships to break the German defenses before the soldiers land on the beach. You will have one month to get ready for the battle." The commander laid out the battle plans on a table for the soldiers to look at. After familiarizing themselves, John and Brody walked back to their assigned tent and went to bed because they had a long training day ahead of them the next day.

"Wake up!" yelled the officer. "You boys better be ready for training. Head out to the yard after you've eaten breakfast." John went to the cafeteria and got in line. Then he sat down with Brody.

"How do you think today's training is going to go?" Brody asked.

"Rough, judging from the commander's battle-plans."

John walked to the yard to get ready for training. The commander yelled "Today's training will be brutal. We will have target practice then go through a lot of exercises." After training John went back to the tent to get some new clothes before lunch.

After one month, the commander walked outside the tents and shot a rifle to wake up the troops. As John woke, Brody asked him, "Are you ready?"

"Yeah, but this is going to be rough on all of us." John responded. As John and Brody walked to the ships, they saw soldiers receiving rifles and ammo. John and Brody walked to their ship, along with thousands of other soldiers, some walking to their deaths.

"Get to the docks! This is what we've been training for men!"

"Do you think we can make it out of this?" John asked Brody.

"I'm not sure. The Germans probably put traps all over that beach." John and Brody walked into the hull of the battleship from which the army would launch the tanks and troop carriers.

As the Nazi soldiers hurried to set up their fortifications and fox holes, they tried everything to stop any invasions from the allies. Meanwhile the American battleships were departing from the docks.

"Commander, the ships must stop. There's a storm ahead!" the communications officer said.

"Okay, tell all ships to proceed for five miles, then to stop," the commander ordered.

"Yes, Sir!"

As the ships came to a stop, they radioed back to port with their progress. While the ships were at a halt, the crew members tended to the cannons, making sure there were no jammed guns and preparing for the bombardment they were about to unleash.

Meanwhile, the Germans had intercepted the radio message from the ships, but they didn't know that the "storm" wouldn't come.

"Commander! The storm has cleared early so we can continue the charge!" the communications officer reported.

"Tell all ships, Full steam ahead!"

As the battleships came into the sights of a terrified German scout, he yelled, "The American's are here!" but it was too late. A fire erupted as the shells from an allied battleship slammed into a German bunker. Fear struck into the hearts of the German soldiers as the massive American battleships appeared out of the fog. As the ships destroyed the fortifications, troop carriers loaded with soldiers started departing from the battleships. John and Brody stepped into one of the many troop carriers. They each said a prayer for their and fellow brothers' safety during the intense battle that was about to happen.

"400 yards away!" yelled the boat's gunner. A terrified John sat in silence. "Hey John, you good?" asked Brody.

"Yeah," John said.

"We're going to make it out of this alive," said Brody.

"300 yards," yelled the gunner. "200 yards away. 100 yards! Get ready for landing!" As the ship slammed into the shore, its door opened. The German machine gunners immediately targeted them. John fell into the water as his fellow

soldiers fell to the ground after being shot.

"John, get up!" Brody yelled as he dragged John out of the water. "Come on, we've gotta go now. They're shooting at us. Come on!" John got up, and they hurried to a nearby fox hole that had some other soldiers in it.

"What are we going to do?" asked one of the soldiers.

"We need to wait for the tanks," another said.

"Look, there's a small trench over by that bunker!" another soldier yelled. Everyone got up and ran to the trench. Luckily, they all made it without getting hit.

"We need to get up the hill. If we do, then it's over for the Germans."

 John yelled. "Someone stay back and give us cover fire." All the soldiers got up and ran to the hill as fast as they could.

"Watch out--there around the corner," yelled a soldier. A few soldiers turned around the corner and caught the Germans by surprise.

"Clear the way. Flamethrower coming through!" yelled a commander, as a soldier with a flamethrower came up. He walked up to the side of the bunker entrance and fired the weapon inside. The whole bunker was immediately engulfed in flames. All the German soldiers went flying out the mouth of the bunker. By this time, the soldiers had made it up the hill and secured most of the beach.

*****

"We›ve finally completed the mission," the commander yelled.

"This feels a little too good." John said.

"Come on John. We completed the mission and made it out alive, so let's be happy that we've been this lucky." Brody answered. Soldiers started to set up medic tents. Those could still fight would keep going to Berlin.

"Come on, let's enjoy this time before we go to Berlin," Brody said.

"Ok, I guess we should. After all, we are in France so we should enjoy

ourselves."

"Ok men, we're getting ready to go through town. Prepare the tanks and get moving!" a soldier yelled. The soldiers got into their armored vehicles, and the foot soldiers climbed on the back of tanks. As the heavy vehicles approached the town, the French civilians cheered for the soldiers and gave them food and drinks. John, who was sitting on the back of a T26E1-1 tank next to Brody, was happy.

"This is nice, huh?" Brody asked.

"Sure is!" John said. All the soldiers were having a good time, nothing could go wrong…right?

"Get ready, I think they›re coming!" yelled a German tank commander. A few Tiger tanks emerged from some bushes. The Germans were planning to catch the American tanks by surprise. As the steel monsters came out of cover, they came upon a farmer. The farmer stood there in shock.

"I have to warn the Americans." He started to run but the Germans were already aware of him. The tank started to shoot its 50-cal machine gun at him, but he got away.

"Nazis, Nazis!" yelled the man as he ran towards the allied tanks. The man went up to the lead tank and yelled at the driver, "There are several German tanks up around the corner!" As the French man was yelling at the tank crew, out of nowhere, a Tiger appeared behind a jeep in the back of the armored division. Everyone was in shock. The commander of the lead American tank was staring into the Tiger's massive 88mm gun.

Seconds later, a deafening clang rang through the town. The Tiger had shot a jeep and destroyed it. All the American tanks struggled to move in the tight area of the town to get into a good position to shoot back. Seconds later the Tiger fired its massive 88 again. There was a loud clang, as it bounced off the thick frontal turret of the last T26E-1. The crew of the last tank in the formation immediately took action and fired its 90 mm gun right at the Tiger's turret ring. Moments later the Tiger burst into flames as the turret went flying into the air sky high. The beast was silenced for good.

As the shocked tank crews moved their tanks back into position, the lead tank gave the command to slowly move forward. The lead tank came to a halt at the corner and turned its turret so its gun would face around the bend.

"Slowly move around the corner and kill any Nazis." the commander said. The lead tank turned around the corner. To their surprise, they found the remaining thirteen Tiger tanks faced away from them. "We've caught them by surprise!" the commander whispered to himself. He ordered the rest of the T 26E-1s to line up so they could shoot at them.

Meanwhile, John and Brody took cover inside an abandoned building. "We got this. Our tanks caught them by surprise." Brody whispered.

As the rest of the T26 E-1 tanks moved into position, the lead tank commander radioed the rest of the tanks. "Get ready to unleash hell!" The lead tank fired its 90mm cannon. The silence was gone in an instant as the shells flew through the air. The shells slammed into one of the Tigers, destroying it and penetrating all the way through the tank, then slamming on the 2nd Tiger's turret ring, breaking it. As the Tiger crew panicked, trying to repair its turret ring, the other German tank crews realized they were under attack. Unfortunately for the damaged Tiger, the lead T26 E-1 loaded another shell into its chamber and fired directly at it. The tank immediately burst into flames. Then the turret flew off the rest of the tank several feet into the air.

As the remaining Tigers got into position, the American tanks fired another volley. Unfortunately, the high explosive shells bounced off the Tiger's thick armor and flew into the buildings, making them fall down. The Tigers returned fire with a loud bang as the German shells flew across the alley, all five striking the lead Tank. The German-made shells were not enough to stop this American beast.

The German shells struck the T26E-1, sending sparks everywhere. Seconds later, the four external fuel tanks ignited from the sparks and caused a massive explosion. Smoke began to fill the air, making it impossible to see. The German tank crews were astonished to see the American tank roll out of the smoke as if it were untouched. Fear struck into the hearts of all the Tiger tank crews.

"It's invincible!" one of the German commanders yelled into the radio.

All the soldiers' jaws dropped as they watch this happen. "Wow Brody! These new prototypes the general bought sure are tough!" John said. Brody stared at the T26 E-1 in amazement.

"I guess so," Brody responded.

"We need to get out of here," one of the soldiers said.

"Yeah, or we'll be turned into pancakes," another said. All the men got up and exited out of the back of the building. They ran into a fox hole to take cover.

"How much longer is this battle going to go on? I mean our Pershings are super strong, but there are at least a dozen Tigers left," Brody said.

"I don›t know, but let's hope luck is on our side today," John said.

The remaining Tigers finally maneuvered back into a good position, angling their 100mm armor. All the tigers unleashed hell as they fired back. The lead American tank was right in the Tigers path. All ten of the shells slammed into the T26E-1's frontal armor, but none of the shells penetrates. The German tank crews were devastated as they watched the lead T26E-1 fire back.

The shell went through the lead Tiger's lower plate, going all the way through, then penetrating the second Tigers turret and causing its ammo rack to explode.

The last Tiger's commander radioed the rest saying, "Fall back, we can't beat them." The Americans were relieved as they saw a white flag pop out of every working German tank. John whispered to himself "We can go home Now." All the soldiers were amazed at the fact that this battle was easily won, but not a drop of American blood was shed.

The Bear and Wolf

By Adrian Erd

Age 13

By the side of the road in the mountains leading to a secret science lab, a wolf and a bear were enjoying their day, happily chasing grasshoppers together in the green grass. It was a bright day with a nice cool breeze ruffling their fur, but soon this would come to an end.

The wolf slipped away for a moment, but when he returned, his friend was gone. *Well, he must be at the den*, he thought to himself. The wolf walked through the moist grass between huge trees looking everywhere for his friend. The bear wasn't in his bed of sticks and leaves; he wasn't scratching on the seven big rocks that he had marked up with his itching paws. *Maybe he is at the pond*, the wolf thought.

The small pond was fed by an upper pond where a family of six little frogs lived. When the wolf got there, the bear was nowhere to be seen there either. Then, out of the corner of his eye, the wolf noticed his friend in a torn-up net being carried across the rocky road into the lab. He had to do something, so he started to run as fast as he could. Before he made it into the lab, the doors shut on him. He heard men shouting and ran around to the back of the lab just in time to see a supply truck being unloaded. He squeezed through an opening in the fence and slipped into the garage.

He looked around and saw a desk next to a shelf and a door with a large window. He jumped onto the desk and managed to pull himself to the top of the shelf with one paw. He hit the window with his head once. Nothing. He hit it a second time. Still nothing. He pounded the window a third time, finally shattering the glass. He jumped through the broken window and picked his way through the broken glass. He headed down the hall toward two glass doors that, to his surprise, automatically opened when he got near them. He jumped back, full of fright, but then he came to his senses and walked in.

A table stood next to a counter covered with glass tubes full of yellow, blue, and green chemicals. His friend, the bear, was asleep in a cage next to a table. The wolf made a small noise but the bear did not wake up. The wolf looked a little closer to see an empty glass tube attached to a metal needle on the table. He reached through the bars of the cage to scratch the bear, trying to wake him. Then he jumped onto the table and accidentally knocked a glass of water onto the bear.

The bear suddenly woke up in attack mode, but when he saw that it was his friend, the wolf, he calmed down. The glass doors slid open, and two men entered the room. The wolf tried to make a run for it, but slipped on the floor and crashed into the table, causing the chemicals to spill all over both animals.

The pair started to rapidly grow. Their muscles got bigger and huge veins popped out. The lab experts took a good long look at each other, then both started running as fast as they could. The bear and the wolf grew into huge beasts with razor sharp claws. They gained invincibility and battle knowledge, as well the ability to never run out of stamina. The wolf had the power to summon an undead wolf army out of the wounds in his own body. His cells could make an infinite number of undead wolves. The bear could make the earth split in half or make huge earthquakes to destroy everything around him.

They lost control and destroyed the lab. The bear caused an earthquake. The wolf summoned the undead wolf army which wreaked havoc on the area around them. A surviving citizen who lived in the neighborhood called the police, but when the police got there, both animals were gone.

They were headed toward the big city in a tackle formation to hit the buildings. The police saw them and called in the military. As they reached the edge of the city, the military began shooting at them. The undead wolf army started attacking them; the military front line didn't last long.

The army hooked a tank to a Cargobob (a helicopter capable of lifting a vehicle) and flew high in the air. From the air, the tank fired at the bear, hitting him right in the face. He shrugged it off. He and the wolf got distracted by nineteen more flying tanks. They both jumped into the air as the wolf called more undead wolves from his cells. The wolves fell into the Cargobobs, making them crash. The undead wolves went down with them and were all killed. The bear made himself into a cannonball formation and hit four more buildings, knocking them into rubble. The rest of the Cargobobs lifted back up and separated into a circle, surrounding the bear and the wolf. The bear grabbed a boulder and crushed it into smaller boulders and threw them at the rest of the Cargobobs.

The military's last resort was to send the monsters up to space to destroy other planets. They called one more Cargobob and sent it to the edge of space. Before it could ascend, the monsters jumped onto the Cargobob. Destroying it, the bear came rushing down to the ground. Next, the wolf fell down right next to the bear. They got up from the ground and shook themselves. The two destroyers looked down at the city and smiled, as the police were moving people away from the city.

The wolf summoned even more undead wolves. The enormous bear tripped and fell on the skyscrapers, destroying them. The military called in their fastest speed jet. It fired ten missiles at the bear and then at the wolf to get their attention. It worked.

The jet pilot was going to take one for the team. He knew what he must do. He flew straight up in the air. The bear and the wolf jumped as high in the air as they could, and they made it into low-earth orbit. The jet pilot ejected at just the right time before the jet got crushed by gravity pulling in fifteen different directions. The wolf and bear tried to get back to Earth, but they couldn't because gravity pulled them to Mars. To this day, they are out there, known as the Planet Destroyers.

There were 178 deaths on that sad day, and 1.7 billion dollars' worth of damage was done to the city. The government ordered the military to use a device to clear everyone's mind. Their cover up was that a huge earthquake had happened. The labs were banned from making those chemicals, and everything went back to normal on Earth.

The bear and the wolf are still in space destroying planets. They came back to their senses and are best friends once again.

Bag Boy and E-Box

By Luis Dante Munoz

Age 12

Guud Factory makes toys to sell in P&J Toy stores. One night in the Factory, two magic toys appeared. They were alive! One was a Bag Boy who was about the size of a person's hand. The second was E-Box, a cube that could change its size. They were sent to P&J Toys to the section called Craft World.

"Ughhh…" grunted Bag Boy. "Aren't there any people here? Well, I'm lost!"

"Me, too," said E-Box.

"Who are you?" asked Bag Boy with surprise.

"I am E-Box. And you?"

"I am Bag Boy"

"Cool," responded E-Box.

They started exploring but saw no one. They asked each other, "Are We stuck?" They ran to the end of the world and saw the end of Craft World.

"Are we TOYS?!" they asked. They panicked, and E-Box fell to the ground because he had fainted. Bag Boy carried him back to where they had been.

"Ugh….Where am I," said E-Box?

"Shhh. Be quiet. We are toys, and people want us because we're magic!" said Bag Boy.

"Oh," said E-Box. So now they had to hide because people wanted them. After they talked for a bit, they got out of the store, then ran to explore more of the world. The owners of the P&J Store saw the moving toys on the camera by the front door, so they went to find the toys.

Bag Boy went to a coffee shop to see what was inside. He was surprised at the delicious smells. He loved it. E-Box was happy because Bag Boy was happy. Bag Boy wanted a coffee, but he said to E-Box that they were toys, and the people were going to look for them. E-Box had an idea to sneak into where the workers made the coffee, so they did. Bag Boy got goofy, so he said he wanted to mess up people's coffee. E-Box wanted to stop him but it was too late.

"Stop, please. You just wanted coffee," said E-Box, but he could not stop Bag Boy's trolling mood. He made a mess.

"We're dead," said E-Box.

"Yup….ulp," gulped Bag Boy. Someone was coming. Bag Boy ran to hide, and E-Box ran too. They were quiet while the people looked for something. The two owners of the toy store came in because someone had posted on the internet that two magic toys were on the loose in the coffee shop.

Bag Boy saw on the TV that people were searching for them, and he was really sad. He cried in tears, and E-Box said, "It's okay. We have each other." Bag Boy smiled.

When they left out the side of the coffee shop, they found a game store. Bag Boy thought there were more toys like them in the store because game stores have cartoon characters on their posters. Bag Boy ran inside. When he opened the door, he saw so many things that he began running everywhere. Then he saw a person and grabbed E-Box. They ran and hid, but E-Box said that he thought this person may be different. When they talked to him, he was so happy to see walking toys. "It's so nice to meet you," he said because the person played a lot of games. He ran to grab a lot of gift cards and gave them to E-Box. Bag Boy was surprised.

They went back to P&J Toys because they were afraid they would get captured. They lived for a long time at Craft World.

Public Service Warning 2055: Man-Eating Cars

By: Gavin Taylor

Age 14

Man-eating cars have been spotted and are looking for living prey. They like to find people, children, or animals to feast on. The only clue to know when they are near is the sound of a distorted car horn in the distance. During the day, they hide in abandoned buildings such as old schools, barns, houses, and office buildings. Their only weakness is silver. When they are in contact with silver, it melts them from the skin to the axle.

They have three rows of teeth, and three eyes. They can't see very well, so they can only manage to attack things that move quickly. The cars can climb up buildings to scout for children. If a car sees a child, it will roar and start to run after the child. Any child who finds himself in this situation is pretty much dead, because no one can outrun these carnivorous machines.

At night, they stalk their prey from the shadows. Then, when their prey is alone, they are silent, catch their prey, and end their lives. They will catch them and eat them alive. They start by eating the organs, such as the lungs or heart. They like to keep the brain for last. They are mostly found in towns or cities and are usually very rare models.

If you see one of these cars, do not panic. Calm yourself, and slowly walk away as quietly as possible.

Klatavo's Trip to a New World

By Kara (AK) Evans

Age 15

Klatavo was just your average fifteen-year-old alien living on Alpha Centauri. She was not special in any spectacular way, and Klatavo just lived her life doing what she was told when she was told to do it. Klatavo may not have done anything remarkable in the fifteen years she had been alive, but she had grand dreams of adventure, danger, and love. Though she treasured her moments alone to imagine these things, never did she think that any of them would come to fruition. One day, however, that is exactly what happened.

Excerpt from the Diary of Klatavo

Day 10 of the 5ᵗʰ cycle in the 23ʳᵈ Klarien year of Alpha Centauri.

Dear Diary, today was incredible! Today my dreams finally came true! I've spent years wanting and waiting for something wonderful to happen, and now it has! Today, I went to another planet! I went to a planet called E-arth. This planet is so strange. Well, I should probably explain how I got there before I tell you of this strange world. It all started yesterday…

I was minding my own business walking to science class, when my professor tapped me on the shoulder. "You have the top score in the group, so I am giving you a chance to see something new. If you would like, you can skip today and go see a new spacecraft."

"Are you kidding? See a new spacecraft? Of course I want to!" I said. My spirits lifted. Maybe this was the beginning of exciting things starting to happen in my life. I had no idea how right I was.

When I arrived at the place where the spacecraft was docked, I was given a visitor's ID card and led out to see the new achievement of the Nuvato race. The spacecraft was huge, bigger than the structures around the colony center. "Wow!" I said, looking up at it.

"Would you like to see the interior, Miss?" an instructor asked.

"Yes!" I burst out.

"Well, then. Follow me," the instructor said,

walking toward the climbable bricks that led the way into the spacecraft. I was shocked when I entered the craft and the steel exit flaps closed, sealing me inside. The craft then entered a launch sequence. I only had a few moments to strap myself in before the spacecraft began to fly into the deep reaches of space.

It took only one rotation of time to reach the destination programmed into the self-steering computer on the craft. As the craft landed on the surface of the planet, a 3-D image appeared in front of me with the word E-arth on it. In a flash of light, the mechanical atom mover transported me into what seemed to be one of the inhabitant's dwelling structures.

Hard, flat, standing structures surrounded me on four sides. These things (that I can only assume are walls) had a texture to them unlike the completely smooth walls of my home world. They were smooth, yet bumpy when I ran my hand along them. I was sitting on a soft thing. This thing was large enough to lay on. I wondered if it was used like the sleeping mats of Alpha Centauri. There was a rectangular thing hanging on the wall. It must have been some sort of magic; I could see myself in it. Something round above me seemed to be the source of light here. A small creature was living there. It looked like a smaller version of the dragons back home. This world was full of magic. A portion of what I assumed to be a wall allowed me to see outside this structure.

As I sat and looked around, I realized that, as incredible as this was, I should not have been there at all. Who had locked me in the shuttle? Who was responsible for sending me here? I thought about it and had decided to return to the spacecraft, when all of a sudden, there was another flash of light, and the mechanical atom mover transported me back onto the craft. The self-steering then powered on, and I was off, heading back towards home.

When I returned, the instructor was waiting for me. "How did you enjoy your surprise?"

"Wait, is that what that was?" I asked, looking at her.

"Yes. Your professor told us you would enjoy it, so we made it happen."

"Well, I sure did enjoy that! When can I go again?"

"Maybe someday, but not now."

With that, my adventure was over, but I still get to remember it by reading what I have written in this diary. That's all for today. I'll write more tomorrow.

Before the King

By Charissa Fryberger

I have come here to pray before the High King of Heaven. Panting from the exertion of climbing the steep stairs past flocks of huddled and dripping pigeons, I reach the immense front door and step out of the pouring rain into the foyer of His great cathedral. I gaze about in deep awe. Paneled in rich, dark wood with creamy marble floors, this elegant narthex is stunning in every detail. I pause to breathe, listening to the quiet trickle of the ivy-covered fountain recessed into the side wall.

As my eyes grow accustomed to the soft interior light, I make out two maple doors across from where I have entered—great slabs of wood inlaid with delicate images from the life of Christ. They stand at attention, guarding the passage into His sanctuary. My tiptoed steps echo a bit as I cross the marble toward them. The doors are heavy, extending three times my height, but perfectly balanced. I pull one of them open just a crack, enough to peer inside.

I stop short in wonder.

The sanctuary stretches the length of an airplane runway before me. The walls are paneled in the same rich wood, but the floors inside blaze with colors from a luminous marble pavement carefully arranged in elaborate mosaics. Shimmering stained glass windows run up each wall, and pillars soar to great heights, drawing my eyes into the ethereal. At the front of the cathedral, broad, marble steps trimmed in gold lead up to an enormous throne where sits… my King.

He is dressed in silks the colors of jewels, and around His shoulders hangs a radiant cape embroidered with gold and copper thread unlike any fabric I've ever seen. It spills down the steps and fills the sanctuary like a billowing sail. Behind Him, the golden pipes of an extraordinary organ ascend toward the lofty ceiling. The King sits surrounded by angels and apostles, as well as those who have kept the faith and honored Him with their lives. His Son stands by His side. I recognize Him: my Lord and my Friend. His robe, seamless and made from the softest wool, also glows with power and warmth. The King and His Son converse quietly.

Though I try to remain unobtrusive, the King glances my way and notices me peeking through the door. He motions for me to come in. My heart begins to beat faster. This is what I came for—to see Him, to speak with Him—yet now that I'm here, I'm not so sure this was a good idea. How can I face Him? How can I presume to talk to Him?

I am not among those who have kept the faith. Often, I have turned aside, distracted by a myriad of earthly inventions. Because I have been concerned with myself, I have missed opportunities to listen to the cares of others. I have been defensive, sometimes striking out in anger or fear. I have forgotten to ask His advice and His direction, deteminedly setting out on my own paths, then being surprised when they come to dead ends. I have known about Him, wondered at Him, worshiped Him…but not always followed. Now that I'm here, what can I say to Him?

Again, He beckons me to come in.

I look down at my ragged skirt. My blouse is in tatters with a coffee stain down the front. I fiddle with a glove I found lying in the street outside. My dripping shoes are rapidly causing a shallow pool to form on the marble at my feet. This is the best I have, but I am certainly not dressed for an audience with the King. Perhaps I should change my mind. I consider turning to flee, but He beckons me a third time. Slowly, I slip through the narrow opening and turn toward the throne. Awkwardly, I walk down the center aisle. Silently, a million—no, more than a million—countless eyes watch my quiet progress.

I stop at the bottom of the steps, unable to move closer. I do not belong here, and yet here I stand, looking up into the face of the King. Out there in the street, I felt confident and strong. I held my head up, ready to face with pride whatever came, but here I am undone. In the light of His glory, I view myself more truly. My inadequacies are obvious for all to see. I've come empty-handed, with nothing to offer my King.

This cannot end well.

I cannot speak. I have no words to express my sorrow. Melting into a puddle of tears, I fall to my knees, keeping my eyes on the cold stones before me. Suddenly, I am immersed in warmth. It flows over me, through me. Pouring over my matted hair and engulfing my tired body, it splashes onto the floor around me. It leaves me clean and refreshed. My ashen hair turns blonde again. The filth is gone from my skin. Even my fingernails are no longer grimy. I look up. My Lord stands by my side with a dove cooing quietly on His shoulder.

I am left kneeling, unclad before Him, my ragged clothes having been washed away in the deluge. I am clean, but naked and poor in spirit.[1] Those rags were all I had; I have no virtue of my own with which to cover myself.

I still have nothing to offer Him.

But He does not leave me exposed for long. In an instant, my Lord leans down and sweeps His robe around my shoulders. I am completely covered. It feels soft and clean and warm—comfortable—as if this is what I was always meant to wear. My face shines above the soft wool as I look up once again into the eyes of the King. He smiles, no longer seeing the shamed and tattered girl who slipped through the door into His chamber, but rather, one He loves, richly arrayed in the finery of His Son and joyfully bearing His own image. Jesus takes my elbow and gently helps me to stand.

"Welcome, my child," the King says. "You've come home. Come. Sit with me."

With His arm around my shoulder, my Lord escorts me up the steps and, with a smile, presents me to His Father. The King looks deeply into my soul and delights in the Truth He placed in my inward being.[2]

"Sit down with me," the King repeats. "We have much to say to each other." And He begins to teach His wisdom to my secret heart.[2]

NOTES:

[1]Matthew 5:3 ESV.

[2]Psalm 51:6 ESV.

POETRY

Mary in A Martha's World

By Charissa Smith

Sometimes I feel torn in two:
I want to pray, but I've got so much to do!
My heart and soul love Jesus, my King,
but all I hear is the cell phone ring…
I want to sit quietly at His feet each day,
meditating on goodness, in His presence to stay.

I'm half Mary, but half Martha too.
My personality feels split in all I do.
I want to sit at His feet and soak in His power,
but Martha says, "You'll be late; you've an appointment
       in an hour."
Mary calls me to come rest from the chores;
Martha tells me I need to run to the store.

I've a To Do list that is a mile long;
many of you can sing this same song.
Frustration and guilt as the two sisters fight;
inside my heart it is such a sight.
One day Martha is running the show
with Mary shoved out, her Bible in tow.
Next day finds Mary, all humble and meek,
"Lord, You know it's Your will that I seek."

Can you relate to this daily tug of war?
Quick, give me an answer; don't tell me the score.
Bills to pay, and the house is a mess.
How can I survive under all this stress?
The news in the nation is always bad.
It affects my life and makes me sad.

Conflict and fighting is all I hear.
Lord, we know the end is near.
Looking into the future, I don't like what I see.
God, Who sits above all this, please take care of me.
Let Mary win this daily tug of war,
for time in Your presence does my peace restore!

Let My Life

By Abbey Hawn

Let my life be like a seed
planted in the ground
that what may seem invisible,
faithful may be found.

Let my life be like a tree
bearing fruit so sweet
that from what took years to grow,
others now may eat.

Let my life be like a brook,
bubbling oh so clean
that many thirsty travelers
might find a drink in me.

Let my life be like a star,
blazing rays of light.
Let my life be beams of hope
shining through the night.

Untitled

By Lee

Wake up little lamb;
the earth is brand new.
Sing and dance
in the morning dew.
Run and play
in the fields of green.
Feel the cool breeze
as you lay by the stream.
Drink from the river
when you thirst from the sun.
Sleep under the stars
when the day is done.
Dream of a home
where love never fades,
warm in the arms
of the One from whom you're made.
Safe and free,
another's blood has been given.
Rejoice little lamb;
your Savior has risen.

The Wolf

By Amy Munoz

Age 15

In the absent light,
the distant voice of the wolf
becomes the night wind.

Frozen paw prints left
by a creature passing through;
proof that you were here.

Whispers

By Giovanni Rivas

Age 13

Whispers in the wind,
nature's secrets softly shared;
harmony surrounds.

There Once was a Cat...

By: Sarah Brotherton

There once was a cat named Bailey,
who went to the garden daily.
He tried to catch a mouse,
but only found a grouse,
so, he just played his ukulele.

The Love of Nature

By Daniel Everett

Age 16

The grass, the rocks, the trees;
have you ever wondered who created these?
So many different beautiful birds
truly make me feel like I've run out of words.
Even when it's windy and cold, and I'm bored,
I always remember to give thanks to the Lord.

Abba

By Charissa Fryberger

I go looking for God
calling out, "Come, Lord,"
and a voice answers:
"I Am here."
I turn toward the sound
and find Him enthroned,
encompassing the stars,
which are the work of His fingers,
yet mysteriously encompassed by them
as they encircle His shoulders
like glittering, celestial fireflies.
He sits above all
looking over all
illumined by a light
beyond the sun.
He reaches out a colossal hand to me.
I squeal, "Abba!"

His great face beams with delight
as He stoops to greet me.
Laughing, I run up to His knees;
laughing, He receives my tiny embrace.
He lifts me into His lap
and lets me play
with the diamonds and
sapphires
 that adorn his fingers.
His stars twinkle above us,
winking at each other
as I grow tired and lay my head
in the gentle hand
of the King of all creation,

    ...my Daddy.

Song of the Lily Bud

By Abbey Hawn

I'm just a little bud
surrounded by green leaves,
but when my story's done,
a lily I will be.

I may look little now;
you may not notice me,
but over time I'll grow,
and one day you will see.

And when my debut comes,
my beauty will amaze
the eyes of all who see,
and I'll recall the days

when I was not at all
the joy of any eyes,
but somehow all along,
I still held a surprise.

My worth did not begin
the day my colors bloomed,
my beauty hidden there
before the others knew.

The beauty in each heart
begins before you see,
and with each passing day,
it starts to bloom like me.

Humble

By Lee

Why are you hiding, little red rose?
Surrounded by others,
taller they grow.
Yet, you remain small
in a garden so grand,
overshadowed by stature,
blocking the Son from the land.
Do you hold a secret?
Reason to refrain?
While all of the others
dance in the rain?
They're always reaching,
never touching the sky,
but you little rose,
know the reasons why.
For if you stay humble,
your garden will bloom,
and the Son that you seek
will flow out like perfume.

Conversations with God

By Lee

I said, "It's like you got it backwards, Lord. You reward me for doing wrong."

Then He said, "Imagine what I can do when you do right."

The Challenge

By Andrea Wade

Today Satan challenged me
and knocked me to my knees.
He pitched his dirty lies at me
and caused my heart to freeze.

You are dirty; you are unworthy.
You are pitiful and meek.
You are small; you are unfaithful.
You fail when you are weak.

I closed my eyes and gripped my chest,
hearing the onslaught of hate.
He ripped at me and gnawed on me,
hoping I'd take the bait.

The insults were not new;
I'd heard them all before.
His methods had not changed
as his affronts continued more.

I gulped in air and lowered my head,
bearing down upon my knees.
Take these lies away from me.
Lord, give me a reprise!

Thank you for this trial.
 Thank you for your love.
 Thank you for your blessings,
 continually raining from above.

 Help me through this challenge;
 I can't take it anymore.
 Don't let me go back there;
 I remember this from before.

I prayed for reminders,
reminders of who I am.
I prayed for His help
and the coming of the lamb.

Satan felt my armor shift.
He doubled down on the attack.
Anger pulsed through him,
As he searched every nook and crack.

 You haven't talked to Him in weeks;
 your sins are far too great.
 He won't listen to your pleas.
 you are linked to your fate.

My heart broke with these new attacks,
wondering if they were true,
knowing I had not sought forgiveness,
as I know I should always do.

Staying still, afraid to ask,
unsure of what the Lord would say,
I tried to think and remind myself,
Jesus took these sins away.

> Lord, I'm scared to seek you,
> knowing what I've done.
> I'm afraid of my unworthiness
> and the stripes I put on your Son.
>
> Child do not fear.
> I am here, and you may rest.
> He's shaken you and challenged you,
> telling you, you are not blessed.
>
> Stay still my dear one;
> you need not do more.
> I will always fight for you.
> I have already won this war.
>
> This is just a test,
He whispered in my heart.
> A challenge, an attack
> to tear and rip us apart.

But you are not alone.
I am here, as I've always been.
There is nothing too big for me.
Peace, my child. I will win.

The oppression of the evil one
immediately lifted from my soul.
God had returned everything
Satan had so painfully stole.

My strength returned, and I stood again,
lifting my hands in praise.
His truth and love washed over me,
cleansing me in many ways.

Satan's lies were wiped away.
His strength had all run dry.
The challenge was now over.
The Lord's truth reigns on high.

Bored with Miracles

By Charissa Fryberger

What was once an impossibility
    became a rare and awe-inspiring miracle
        on the day Orville was lifted
            into the clear North Carolina sky.

But now we have forgotten the wonder.
    Now we wait boredly;
        we board boredly;
            we stow our bags and sit down—boredly.

We stare straight ahead
    or into our phones,
        not even acknowledging the fact
            that we are defying gravity!

We are no longer thrilled
    to find ourselves
        lifted from the Earth
            and soaring heavenward.

I fear...
    we may have become bored also
        with the One
            Who lifts our souls to Heaven.

Calvary

By Lee

A hill in the distance,
outside of the gate,
passed by each day,
awaiting ill fate.
A well-traveled road,
a well-beaten path,
awaiting the traveler
Who will travel it last.
Two beams of wood
of cedar and pine,
made for the One
Who left ninety-nine.
Thorns on a branch,
wrapped round and round,
made for a King,
worn as a crown.
A love so deep
that day becomes night.
In my sorrow and grief,
a death becomes Life.

A prayer for the Beginning

By Andrea Wade

Lord my heart hurts.

It hurts for the people
who think they are less.
They believe they are unworthy.

I remember what this feels like.
I remember feeling like I was inferior,
not up to the level of those around me.

Life just kept on passing me by
and I thought it was because I was
dirty, unclean, and not good enough.

I didn't want to muddy Your presence.
I didn't want to put a note of discord
into the beautiful symphony of creation.

I couldn't see how I fit in
I didn't want to mess up everything
because You were "supposed" to love me.

I knew the choices I had made.
My choices were not of You…
they were not even for You.

They were of the world and self-pleasure.
They led to heartbreak and destruction.
My life was in shambles, filled with pain.

But You saw me.

You didn't pass me by.
Even when I turned away,
still, you reached out to me.

Your voice whispered love to me.
Your grace flowed over me
like a fresh, clean shower.

Your mercy cleansed me.
You clothed me in white,
and still, I cried.

I was not worthy of Your glory
or Your presence in my life.
I was a discordant note in Your song.

I had made choices regardless of knowing
who You were and what You wanted for me.
I was passive and weak.

I could not be the prodigal child
You forgave and gave the family ring to.
I was completely and totally filthy.

But You pulled me closer, soothing my soul.
You whispered words of love and peace.
You vowed to never leave my side.

You guided my way when I wavered or got lost.
You were there talking to me and walking with me,
carrying me when I could not stand.

You continued for years,
slowly guiding me with patience,
picking me up when I fell.

As time went on, I began to understand
who I was meant to be,
who I am in You.

I stopped saying sorry for everything.
I began to accept who I am
as You walked with me each day.

I began to celebrate my differences,
the unique way I am,
as a cherished gift from you.

Before I knew it,
I was standing on my own feet seeking You,
asking others to join me,

proclaiming your name
just as the woman at the well did.
You are the great I AM!

So now when I listen to others,
when I hear their sorrow and fear,
when they say they are unworthy,
I remember.

I know how that feels,
The complete sorrow and self-doubt.
I remember the beginning.

Lord, I pray for people who are feeling lost.
I pray for people who feel they are less than.
I pray for Your presence in their lives.

Just as it was for me so long ago,
I pray they are open to Your glory,
and to the words You will guide them by.

I pray they will submit to You and trust You.
Lord, I pray Your grace and mercy over their minds.
I pray You work on them and in them.

Thank You, Lord, for pulling me from that place.
Thank You, Lord, for the trial I went through.
I know You have a plan for my life.

I glorify and praise Your name.

~ Amen

To the Sinner

By Lee

To the faithful, You show Yourself faithful.
To the blameless, You show Yourself blameless.
To the pure, You show Yourself pure,
but to the devious, You show Yourself shrewd (Ps 18:25-26).
From the wicked, You remove Your presence,
for Your eye is too pure to see evil (Hab1:13).
To the proud, You show Your detesting,
but to the humble, You show Your grace.
To the stubborn, You show Your rod,
but to the yielding, You show Your staff.
To those who are flipping over tables,
You show Your righteousness and justice.
To those who are bitter and harbor hate in their hearts,
You show Your kindness and compassion.
To the weak, You show Your strength.
To the poor, You show the riches of Heaven.

To the blind, You show Your light.

To the deaf, You sound Your trump.

To the ignorant, You show Your Word.

To the lost, You show the Way.

To those who speak falsely, You show Your Truth.

To those seeking access, You show Life.

To those who ask, You give Your Spirit (Luke 11:13).

To the brokenhearted, You show Your healing,

To the empty, You show Your fullness.

To those who need a breakthrough,

You show mountains moved.

To the warrior, You show Your shield.

To the underserving, You show Your favor.

To the repenter, You show Your forgiveness.

And to the sinner, You show Your scars.

The Chink in Your Armor

By Andrea Wade

Satan is smart.

He knows what makes you run,

what hurts you,

what brings you joy.

Then he uses that to make you regret.

Regret is the chink in your armor he looks for the most.

If he can make you regret, he can make you forget,

forget you are forgiven for your sin,

forget you are forgiven for your past,

forget you are loved.

If he can find a regret, he will whisper into it,

making something small into something monumental.

Regret can lead to changed behaviors.

Regret makes you forsake what you love the most.

It dresses in a disguise of conviction,

and pours shame over its victims.

Regret is the chink Satan is looking for,

the weak spot in an immaculate suit of armor.

He whispers and watches,

waiting for the crack to appear.

Knowing we are human and flawed,

he smiles when the world tempts us,

when it seems the grass is so much greener on the other side,

or when life has beaten us down,

and we begin to lose hope.

He knows all the telltale signs

of a regret fracture about to form.

He stands in anticipation,

staring intently at the pressure building and building.

He laughs, despite his minions falling all around

to angels fighting for our salvation

because he knows if he can wait it out,

if we begin flirting with his idea,

regret will set in and the fracture will open.

He will slide under our armor and eat us alive.

Our health, our emotions, our love—

all of it will become his playground.

Regret is his tool to keep us from looking to the future,

to make us live in the past.

But you cannot stay there;
You will not be left there.

God will not leave you behind.

He is doing new things.

He makes a way in the wilderness of shame and fear.

He makes rivers in the desert of loneliness.

He has redeemed us.

He has called us by name.

He shines his light on regret and casts the shadows away.

He walks through the flame with you,

promising there will be better days

because we are precious in his eyes.

He will restore us and heal us, so we're not overwhelmed.

God sees the pressure we are under,

and how enticing the world can be,

but he cares for us and loves us.

Regret is not where we should go.

He soothes the pressure with each prayer we breathe.

He coats it in conviction,

not willing for us to fall into the lies,

beckoning us back to him,

not wanting us to feel the hurt from our mistakes.

In forgiveness and mercy, he holds out his hand,

not focusing on what we did.

So don't regret your past;

it's already been forgiven.

Let it go, and give it to him,

so that he can build you the future

you were always meant to have.

Pink Feather

By Lee

I found you along the beaches of Heaven,
while I was adrift in my sin and shame,
desperate for my vindication
from the kindling of my fire's flames.
And there you were,
alone on the shore,
waiting there just for me,
calming the storm,
preparing the way,
renewing my hope,
washing me clean,
declaring my future,
revealing your plan,
while I found peace in your promise,
lying there in the sand.
Then deep called to deep,
so, I prepared for flight
toward your healing redemption,
guided by Love and Light.

A Celebration of Octogenarianism

By Charissa Fryberger

As you celebrate your octogenarian birthday—
plus one—
with your family spread across the nation
like the arms of an octopus—
hmmm…actually we are 16,
so perhaps, like two octopi—
you can watch this tumultuous year
fade into fall.

September gives way to October,
which should,
linguistically speaking,
be the eighth month,
though it is actually the tenth
(we can thank Julius Caesar for that bit of confusion—
though I guess we can't blame him
for the current year's chaos).

Though we are connected only by
an octo x octo electronic face
(wouldn't that be a 64-bit computer?)
and a cell phone octothorp
(more contemporarily known as a hashtag),
I want to wish you a birthday
filled with an octillion of joy
and high-octane laughter.

May you have an octave celebration.
Just don't fall off your octohedron
in the hilarity.
I hope you have a chance
to look into the depth of the night sky
and view an octodecillion array
of twinkling stars
smiling down upon you.

All these octa-symbollic words
make me want to do something octartistic,
like draw a picture made up of octagons
galloping octagonally
across eight sheets of paper;
or play you a song on an octachord
in the company of an octet
(I might need the help of my musical daughter for that one);

or write you a fairytale using octosyllabic words.
I'm not sure how that would go.
Perhaps I could tell a tale about
an antiquated iatromathematician
doing an ethnogeographically bounded analysis
of the Machiavellianistic tendencies
in the orthography of orangutans in the Oman,
but I fear it would turn into a horror story.

So perhaps I'll settle for piecing together
this bit of octonary verse,
Though I'm not quite good enough
to do it in octometer.
O dear, this is but seven stanzas—
a septenary poem just won't do.
But then again—maybe it will be an appropriate nod
To your September birth.

In the midst of this octupling of silliness,
congratulations on completing your first
octogenarian year!

                With Love,
                From your eldest daughter
                (who is merely
                an aspiring octogenarian).

Glossary

Ethnogeographically:	Studying the geographical distribution of races or peoples and their relation to the environments in which they live.
Iatromathematician:	Someone of a school of medicine of the 17th century that explained disease and the activities of the body in terms of physics rather than of chemistry.
Machiavellianism	Philosophical agreement with the writings of 16th century politician Niccolo Machiavelli.
Octachord	Musical instrument with eight strings.
Octagon	Polygon of eight angles and eight sides.

Octagonally	In a way that suggests an octagon.
Octahedron	Solid object with eight faces.
Octane	Any of several isomeric liquid alkanes C_8H_{18}
Octave	Eight-day period of observances beginning with a festival day.
Octet	Musical composition with eight instruments or voices.
Octillion	Number equal to 1 followed by 27 zeros.
Octodecillion	Number equal to 1 followed by 57 zeros. (I have no idea what this has to do with eight)
Octometer	Line of poetry with eight metrical feet.
Octonary	Poetic group of eight verses.
Octopus	Specific type of eight-armed mollusk.
Octopi	Plural of octopus.
Octosyllabic	Words eight syllables.
Octothorp	The pound sign: #. Now known as a hashtag.
Octuple	Multiplied eight times; a sum eight times as great: an eightfold amount.
Octupling	Increasing something eightfold.
Octuplets	Eight babies at the same time—oh the poor mom.
Octartistic	Ok, guilty—I made this one up: an art form based on eights.
Octogenarian	***My Mom.***

ESSAYS AND COMMENTARY

Looking for a pet?

By: Hannah Brotherton,

Age 11

Hi there! Looking for a pet hermit crab? Well, here are five facts about hermit crabs.

First, hermit crabs are social animals. It would be a good idea to get more than one. I have three hermit crabs in a twenty-gallon tank. Their names are Molly, Max, and Mango. They are all friends.

Second, hermit crabs molt under their substrate. While they are molting it is best not to disturb them. My crab, Molly, is currently molting and has been for over a month now. If the hermit crab is large, it could take many months to complete the molting process. If the crab is medium size, it could take one to two months. If the crab is small, it may only take a few weeks to a month.

Third, hermit crabs might fight. Sometimes Max and Mango try to fight. If you see your hermit crabs going head-to-head with an open claw, then they may be starting to fight. Move your crabs to opposite sides of the tank and they should settle down.

Fourth, crabs like all kinds of fruits and vegetables. Be sure to offer them a variety each night. They also like dried river shrimp and coconut flakes. You also need to offer them fresh water and salt water. They like to soak in water.

Finally, don't paint hermit crab shells. The paint can be toxic to the hermit crabs. It is best to buy natural shells for the crabs to live in.

I hope you found these five facts helpful.

An Educated Person in the 21st Century

By Charissa Fryberger

We, who live in the 21st century, are the most educated population that has ever lived…or are we?

Global literacy rates are climbing; more students than ever are finding their way into colleges and universities; and of course, we have the internet. Some say that information which easily crosses international boundaries and arrives before us at the touch of a few keys leads to a broader education for everyone; others bemoan the explosion of information and its corresponding misinformation, suggesting that because it is difficult to discern what is true from what is not, or to wade through the churning opinions that flood our inboxes, we actually know less than in the days when people spent hours pouring over books in a quiet library. Some celebrate the electronic media that lets us delve more deeply into research and study; others complain that the constant interruptions from email and pop-up ads keep us from thinking deeply about anything.

Our global, high-tech world is either blessed with or drowning in billions of gig of data…so, are we more educated then our predecessors? Or less so?…Or does education in the 21st century mean something new entirely?

When universities began to spread across Europe in the late Middle Ages, it was not unusual for someone to hold doctoral degrees in astronomy, philosophy, medicine, and theology, or some other equally disparate set of disciplines. An educated person was learned in a broad range of fields. Today, although people sometimes hold more than one advanced degree, those credentials are usually in in closely related fields. The professors, PhD candidates, and postdocs who wander about the world's campuses every day are experts in their fields, but those fields have become very specialized.

What, then, does it really mean to be an educated person? Does it mean that we've read all the right books? That we speak several languages? That we are degreed and credentialed? That we have written widely-read books or academic papers? Or that we have developed new knowledge in our selected fields?

All of these are elements of education, and means toward becoming educated, but I suggest that they are no longer the criteria for considering someone to be a truly educated person. Each of us sees life—our own, and the lives of those around us—through a particular lens, our own set of assumptions. Like a classic syllogism, we bring together a series of premises and draw from them what we determine to be the best conclusions. However well-informed and carefully taught our own lens may be, it is still but *one* lens, and our one lens may, in fact, be narrow, dusty, incomplete, or flawed.

I suggest that in our 21st century environment, what really distinguishes an educated person is their ability to look beyond their own viewpoint to really understand the perspective of someone else—to see through someone else's lens.

Now this idea of recognizing other perspectives and respecting other people's opinions is neither new nor very unusual. In our society, which is concerned with multinationalism, multiculturalism, multi-viewpoints of every kind, it receives a great deal of lip service in the press, in institutions of higher learning, in business, and in politics—a great deal of lip service, but not so much actual practice. Now, I don't mean to dismiss nor denigrate institutional efforts to help people broaden their perspectives, but in fairness, I don't think that the institutional level is the most effective place to begin in changing our perceptions. This must be done on a personal, one-to-one level.

Most of us start with an assumption that other people think like we do. If we see people doing things or expressing opinions or even wearing clothing different from our own, we often judge them based not on their assumptions, but on our own, which may be vastly different from those that informed their thoughts or behaviors. We judge their actions and ideas based on the premises of our syllogisms, when their conclusions are actually drawn from their own syllogisms.

"What were they thinking?" we say. However, that questions is rarely asked seriously or directed to the person against whom we are making our judgements. Instead, we jump quickly to the conclusion that what they are saying or doing is ridiculous, idiotic, or wrong, when, if we actually knew what they were thinking, we might very well find their conclusions and behaviors to be perfectly reasonable—just as reasonable, in fact, as our own.

Let me offer an illustrative case study: I had a student some years ago when I was teaching in Colorado who, for the purposes of this essay, I will call Allen. He was mathematically brilliant, but because he was on the autism spectrum, he often found himself angry and frustrated with the reactions and behaviors of the people around him. People simply didn't act the way he expected them to. Their emotionally-motivated choices seemed to him irrational, illogical, and inefficient. Allen struggled in any situation in which he had to interact with other people.

Eventually, he decided to study his own condition and read everything he could about it. His epiphany came when he suddenly realized that not everyone thought or processed information like he did. Allen hadn't recognized that there was any other way to assess the world than from his own perspective. Suddenly he realized that other people were drawing their conclusions from an entirely different set of assumptions.

Everyone around him suddenly became a case study. He gradually gathered information about each person until he could forecast their behaviors and know how they would react based on their prevous conduct. Though what they did still often seemed irrational to him, he could now predict their illogic and began to understand their differing assumptions.

Now, seeing other people's behavior as reasonable will never come naturally to Allen. It requires careful diligence and conscious choice to look through other people's eyes. Allen still sometimes sees their choices through the veil of his own judgement and becomes frustrated with what his peers and his teachers do, but other times he is able to consciously choose to look through the parameters of someone else's assumptions.

I suggest that, though he had always been well-read, could do advanced calculus, and often spouted facts on a wide variety of subjects, Allen became an educated individual when he realized that it was possible to approach the people and problems around him from more than one angle. He began to attempt to see through other people's viewpoints and to intentionally honor the perspectives of others, even though he often still disagreed with them.

We have become a very polarized society that is quick to demonize, or at least to idiocize, those whose opinions or beliefs don't conform to our own. Ad ho-minem attacks have become normal fare for politicians, radio talk show hosts, media newscasters, and many Facebook posters. If someone posts an opposing view, we are quick to call them an idiot, or worse, to suggest that they are maliciously trying to destroy__________(fill in the blank).

Both sides of the political spectrum hold sets of requisite views on issues which are not up for debate within the communities of their members. Whether someone is generally a conservative but supports some degree of gun control, or if they self-identify as a liberal but don't buy into some aspects of the feminist agenda, their own political peers—those whom they generally support—often become quick to suspect them, to discount them, or even to demonize them. Arguments quickly become heated, and relationships become strained or broken. It is particularly difficult to see and to honor another perspective if it is not only outside our own, but also outside the understanding of a grand majority of the people with whom we commonly associate.

Most people, however, have reasons behind the personal opinions they hold. If we ask why they think as they do, rather than simply judging them to be the enemy, we might find that they see things from a completely different angle than we do, and that from their angle, the positions on which they stand make sense. We don't have to agree with them on these matters, but we must try to understand that they are coming from a completely different set of assumptions. They may speak from experiences we have never had or viewpoints that have never crossed our minds. Who knows, maybe a conclusion coming from the weaving of my assumptions with theirs could produce a solution to a conundrum that neither of us could solve within the confines of our own limited perspectives.

This quest to understand the assumptions that lead other people to the behaviors or opinions that seem odd or even wrong to us cannot begin with the hot-button issues that rankle emotions and raise walls of defense. Perhaps beginning with a smaller, less world-shaking question may be effective in getting us started. Let me suggest a basic personal exercise which gets us thinking about other people's perspectives, but remains literally "skin deep."

Based on my own opinions (and my age) the idea of getting a tattoo is definitely beyond my ken. However, among younger people where I live in Colorado, tattoos are just short of universal. Some years ago, I became curious about why people chose the images that they had indelibly etched into their skin. I started asking the question of friends and then of strangers—standing in the grocery line, wandering by in the park, sitting at the library. It was a question that drew a wide range of stories and an interesting collection of other people's perspectives. And their choice of permanent images usually made perfect sense, based on *their* assumptions, goals, artistic tastes, personal symbols, and reasons for getting the tattoo in the first place.

A woman in Laramie, Wyoming had the seven dwarfs tattooed across the small of her back. I don't think I would have chosen Happy and Dopey and Sneezy, but she thought they were a perfect fit for her personality.

On an airplane, I sat across the aisle from an older man with a date inked across his wrist. He explained that on their 20th wedding anniversary, he and his wife had gone together to have their wedding date tattooed on their wrists as a symbol of their continuing commitment. Ok, so I'm still not likely to get a tattoo, but his suddenly not only made sense, but seemed sweet and romantic.

As I have implied a couple of times in this writing, to see someone's perspective and recognize the reasonableness of their behaviors or opinions based on their assumptions, may help us respect their choices and ideas, but it does *not* mean that we have to agree with them. We can hold true to our own beliefs while still striving to apprehend the reasons and emotions that lead other people to theirs. Understanding does not require capitulation.

We may, after all, have information they don't have; we may adhere to a different worldview; or our own learning or backgrounds may not produce the same assumptions as theirs. We may even buy into their assumptions and still not agree with the conclusions they have drawn or the choices they have made. Empathy does not require agreement, only the initial presumption that this other human being with whom we are interacting is a reasonable person, not an idiot, a demon, or an enemy.

We might even discover that understanding the viewpoint of someone else will show us how to better articulate our own positions, so that they make sense to our opponents, rather than just raising their walls of defense. Indeed, the art of persuasion is dependent on the art of empathy. To engage in a productive discussion with an adversary, we must first understand their positions, then explore their reasons behind those positions, then find whatever common ground may be available as a place to begin a beneficial and fruitful dialogue. Rather than throwing stones, perhaps we could become not only more educated people, but a more educated community—one that truly does recognize and honor disparate viewpoints, rather than one that only says that it does.

I do not want to suggest that the traditional measures of education—the books we read, the languages we learn, or the degrees we earn—lack value. After all, I am a teacher and have spent more than ten years on college campuses. However, in this world of information overload and polarized opinions, it is of paramount importance that we remember the people behind the news videos, internet tirades, and radically differing opinions that flow by us daily. However the perspectives of others may differ from our own, if we can begin by assuming that what they are saying is reasonable based on *their* assumptions, even if we disagree with them, and then seek to understand those assumptions, we can begin to view our own world through a larger lens. We may be able to give those who currently oppose us a glimpse of the world through our lens as well.

Perhaps then, we really may become the most educated population that has ever lived.

Evidence for God

By Quin Friberg

As we examine the concept of God in this article, I will argue that the biblical description strongly matches the evidence. In order to make that point, let's clarify a few details regarding the biblical understanding of God with reference to the views of various world religions. The God of the Bible, in nature and being, is defined by the following characteristics.

A. Creator of All Things (Genesis 1:1)

God is said to be the creator and cause of the universe, and therefore God would be separate from the universe. God is not the universe, and creation is distinct from the creator in the biblical view of God. This position would not be held in the Hindu, Buddhist, or New Age concepts. These hold a more pantheistic view that all is God. When examined, however, it becomes clear the evidence points to the biblical God, as opposed to a pantheistic or animistic belief.

B. God is Eternal in Nature (Psalm 90:2)

Seeing as the existence of time itself is the fourth dimension of the universe, God, being outside the universe (creation), would necessarily exist in a realm beyond time in eternity. Comprehending a timeless state is impossible for humans because our universe only functions within time. The inability to comprehend, however, has no bearing on the truthfulness of the statement.

C. God is Infinite in Power (Psalm 147:5)

The God of Scripture is not a limited, finite human or demi-god. He is a being of ultimate power and control. We can conclude that if God is able to bring a universe into existence, then the term "infinite in power" would be an appropriate description.

D. God has a Mind and Will (All of Scripture)

In contrast to the deist view in which God is a creator who started the universe and then stepped back, the biblical position claims God is a personal being with a mind and will who is relational by nature. The entirety of Scripture presents this picture, as God communicates with mankind, has a sovereign will and plan, and gives moral obligation. All of this only makes sense regarding a person. The Bible rejects the idea of a universal force or energy as the originator of all things – such as in Star Wars, similar to many Eastern lines of thought.

Now that we have a brief outline of who the God of the Bible is, let's look at four arguments that this God must exist:

Cosmological Evidence for God

We begin our look through the evidence with one of the four historical arguments for the existence of God: the cosmological argument. This argument uses a deductive structure of logic to show there must be a cause for the universe, but not just any cause. Here is the argument in syllogistic form:

> Premise 1: Everything that begins to exist has a cause.
>
> Premise 2: The universe began to exist (i.e., went from not existing to existing at some point).
>
> Conclusion: Therefore, the universe has a cause.

If the two premises presented for this argument are correct, the conclusion necessarily follows. The question becomes, why believe these two premises are true, and therefore the conclusion?

Support for Premise 1: The laws of logic, specifically the law of causality, show us that anything that goes through a transition from one state to another needs a cause for doing so. There is no logical world where A becomes B for no reason and with no law or force acting upon A. If the universe did not exist at some point, and then came into existence at a later point, there must be a reason.

Even atheist physicists and philosophers will agree with this first premise. There are no logical grounds to claim the universe popped into existence with no cause or reason for doing so. One is literally forced into the belief that the universe came from nothing if this premise is rejected. Then one must ask, what is it about nothingness that caused it to produce something? If it truly is nothing, it cannot be the cause of something, because from nothing, nothing comes. Premise 1 can be accepted easily on logical and experiential grounds.

Support for Premise 2: How do we know the universe has not always existed, but instead had a beginning? There are both logical and scientific reasons for the acceptance of Premise 2. First, infinite progression is logically impossible inside the real world. While the idea of infinity may help in math equations, it does not exist in nature. There must be a first, initial cause for all other causes, and this must also be the cause of time itself, since time is part of the fabric of the universe. There must be something or someone outside time that pushes the first domino of cause and effect, because living in a world where everything is an intermediate domino does not make logical sense.

Here is a mental exercise to help demonstrate this. Imagine our universe has always existed, and at the center of the universe there have always been two planets orbiting their star. One planet (named Blue) orbits the star every 50 days, while the other (named Red) orbits every 500 days. Planet Blue orbits the sun ten times faster and more often than Red. The question is, in an infinitely old universe with no beginning, which one has orbited the star more? Mathematically, they would be identical; they have both orbited an infinite number of times. But logic would say that's not correct, because Blue orbits the sun ten times as often. Math of the infinite falls apart in the real world because the infinite is abstract and not part of nature.

If that's not enough, there is now solid scientific evidence to support Premise 2. Scientists have learned that the amount of usable energy in the universe is decreasing, exposing the fact that the universe can't be infinite.

Imagine finding a sealed bottle of water leaking from the bottom onto a counter. How long has the bottle been leaking? One can't say forever, because if it were forever, the bottle would have emptied by the time we saw it. Similarly, the universe is leaking energy, and if it were leaking its limited supply (we know it's limited because the universe is not infinite in size) for an infinite amount of time, it would have leaked all its usable energy by now.

If Premises 1 and 2 are both true, that means the universe must have a cause. But why do we believe God is the best explanation for this cause? Here are a few reasons:

A. The cause must be outside time

Time itself is part of the universe, and whatever caused the universe must necessarily be outside the universe, which also means outside time. God alone fits this description.

B. The cause must be infinite in power

Something caused the entire universe to come into existence, making this cause extremely powerful. The biblical description of God again fits perfectly.

C. God avoids an infinite progression

Remember the two planets and the problem of infinite progression? It turns out the only way to avoid the infinite progression issue is if the cause of the universe is itself outside time – detached from the natural, material state. A popular view has tried to claim that other universes birthed ours. The question then becomes, what birthed those universes? The only solution to solve the infinite progression and maintain a logical position is to appeal to a timeless cause. And the most conceivable timeless cause is God. Additional problems also exist for multi-verse theories.

D. The cause must have a mind and a will

Perhaps the greatest support for God as the cause of the universe is the demand that the cause has a mind and will of its own. Up to this point, one could argue that a force, such as gravity (or Star Wars?) is the cause of the universe, but there's one big hole in that theory. Forces act by law, not by will. Gravity does not choose to make a boy fall back to the ground when he jumps into the air, it just does. Whatever the force does by nature is done without thought.

Remember the water bottle analogy mentioned earlier? If the universe were created by a force, the question becomes: why did the force wait so long to make the universe? If force by nature produced the universe, it should have done so an infinite amount of time ago. The universe should therefore be infinite in age. But we know it's not. The fact the universe is not infinite then requires a mind and a will that chose to wait until a certain point to create the universe. That means the force is personal, which perfectly lines up with the biblical God.

Teleological Evidence for God

The second line of evidence for God comes from the design found in the universe. The argument is called the teleological argument; telos is from the Greek, meaning *purpose*. This line of argument shows things made with obvious purpose must have a designer and intelligence behind them.

Philosopher William Paley gives a classic analogy in support of this argument. Imagine you are walking through a forest. There is no sign of mankind, no evidence that mankind has ever been there, and no historical evidence that anyone has travelled to that forest. But as you walk, you notice something on the ground, a pocket watch. Not only is the watch there, but as you pick it up, you also see it is fully functioning. Whatever you might conclude about how it got there, you certainly wouldn't believe that it had been there forever or that it had simply appeared. Paley, therefore, says the conclusion is simple: someone made the watch. Never would you conclude the watch naturally appeared by random processes – complexity and purpose (telling time) would prevent that conclusion. Without evidence for a watchmaker or watch-owner, you would conclude one exists, because watches don't just come about without intentional, intelligent design.

Here is the technical structure for the teleological argument:

> Premise 1: Fine-tuning and complexity with a purpose implies a designer.
>
> Premise 2: The universe is fine-tuned and complex with a specific purpose.
>
> Conclusion: The universe has a designer.

The term *fine-tuning* is meant to convey the idea of something being tuned for a specific purpose, and in this argument that purpose is life. Philosophers and scientists present the anthropic principle (anthropic meaning life). This points us toward the realization that the universe is literally tuned and designed for the purpose of the existence of life, both on the large scale of the universe and the local scale of the solar system and our planet.

Support for Premise 1: Premise 1 appeals to logic, experience, and mathematics. Logic tells us that organized information meant to accomplish a goal is evidence of design. Experience tells us if you find a complex system designed to fulfill a purpose (e.g., the watch in the forest), it requires an intelligent designer. Mathematics tells us that random chance processes will never produce a complex information system; the statistical odds of random processes doing so is absurd. The conclusion is unavoidable: if the universe is highly complex and geared to fulfill a specific purpose, that strongly implies a designer designed it with that purpose in mind.

Support for Premise 2: The question needing answered, then, is does the universe contain such design? The clear answer is yes. The universe has been fine-tuned for life to exist, and if any one of a number of factors varied, life would be impossible in the universe and on the earth. But don't just take my word for it. Experts in the field agree.

A. The large scale of the universe

1. The Strong Nuclear Force

"Calculations indicate that if the strong nuclear force, the force that binds protons and neutrons together in an atom, had been stronger or weaker by as little as 5%, life would be impossible." (Leslie, 1989, pp. 4, 35; Barrow and Tipler, p. 322)

2. The Gravitational Constant

"Calculations by Brandon Carter show that if gravity had been stronger or weaker by 1 part in

10 to the 40th power, then life-sustaining stars like the sun could not exist. This would most likely make life impossible." (Davies, 1984, p. 242)

If you'd like to see just how fine-tuned that is, and how low the odds of it randomly occurring would be, here is an illustration. Go into space and set a one square foot target on the edge of the universe. Then come back to the earth. Now take a gun, point in any direction, and shoot. The odds of the gravitational constant being randomly correct are roughly the same odds as you hitting the target.

3. Proton-Neutron Ratio

"If the neutron were not about 1.001 times the mass of the proton, all protons would have decayed into neutrons or all neutrons would have decayed into protons, and thus life would not be possible." (Leslie, 1989, pp. 39-40)

4. Electromagnetic Force

"If the electromagnetic force were slightly stronger or weaker, life would be impossible, for a variety of different reasons." (Leslie, 1988, p. 299)

These are just a few snapshots of the large universal picture. Now let's narrow our focus to our local solar system.

B. The local solar system and planets

   1. Oxygen Levels

Oxygen levels must be precise for life to exist on

the earth. Were they too high, forest fires would literally burn out of control and everything would be consumed. Were they too low, life wouldn't be possible.

2. Atmospheric Transparency

The earth's atmosphere accepts and maintains just enough heat from the sun. If our atmosphere were thicker (like Venus), the temperature would rise to hundreds of degrees, and if it were thinner (like Mars), we would freeze to death.

3. Moon-Earth Gravitation

Without the moon in place, the earth's oceans wouldn't experience tides, and all marine life would die. Once ocean life died, oxygen levels would fall and all life would cease to exist.

4. Earth's Rotation

If the earth rotated too fast (like Jupiter), the strong winds would make life impossible. If it rotated too slow (like Mercury and Venus), everything would burn from long days and freeze from long nights.

5. Distance From the Sun

If the earth were too close to the sun, everything would burn up. If it were too far away, everything would freeze. Scientists have called our position the Goldilocks Zone.

Our universe, solar system, and planet all appear to

be designed with one purpose – for life to exist. Since Premise 2 also is correct and design is evident, then the conclusion is correct. An intelligent designer exists who fashioned it all.

The teleological argument shows an intelligent mind had to create the universe, just as the cosmological argument reveals. The teleological argument, however, goes a step further and shows the purpose of creation centers around the existence of life on our planet. The Bible actually states that life is the purpose of the creation and that God created with mankind in mind. We will discuss this point more later in the book.

Ontological Evidence for God

Perhaps no argument is more complicated than the ontological argument when discussing the evidence for God. Many will feel like this one is a trick. But the logical structure is sound, and if the premises are true, the conclusion necessarily follows. If this evidence becomes too difficult to process, continue to the next section. That one will be easier and may enhance your understanding of this one. When one grasps this argument, however, disbelief in God is revealed as ignorance of who He truly is.

The argument was first developed by Anselm of Canterbury in the 11th century. Anselm argued that the existence of God was not only likely, but necessary, and Psalm 14:1 says it's foolish to claim there is no God.

Here are the premises of his argument and his conclusion:

> Premise 1: God is the object of thought of which no object of thought can be considered to be greater.

Now suppose God is only in the intellect (i.e., He exists in the mind but not in reality). But…

> Premise 2: Any object of thought that can be believed to exist in reality will certainly be
>
> thought to be greater than any object of thought that exists only in the intellect.
>
> Premise 3: It cannot be doubted that God can be thought to exist in reality, not only in the intellect.
>
> Premise 4 and Conclusion: Therefore, some object of thought can be thought to be greater than
>
> the object of thought of which no object of thought can be greater, which is a contradiction. And so, we have to abandon our supposition that God is only in the intellect. He must also exist in reality.

Anselm argues God is not simply a being that might exist, but rather by definition, is a being that must exist – He is a necessary being. Instead of going into detail defending each premise, which isn't difficult, we will first look at a modern-day construction of the argument by philosopher Alvin Plantinga.

Before listing the premises and conclusion, let me clarify a few terms. When philosophers speak of *"possible worlds"*, they simply mean a way that reality could be, not necessarily the way reality is. For example, unicorns don't exist, but there is a possible world where they do exist. This means we can imagine a logical world where unicorns are a creature, even if they're not a creature in the real world.

Not every world is possible, though. There is no world where square triangles exist because that is logically and mathematically impossible. A world with black and white rainbows isn't possible either, because rainbows are, by definition, related to the visible spectrum of light. A possible world is a valid description of how the world could logically be.

Next, Plantinga uses the phrase *"maximally great being"*. A maximally great being is infinite in power and knowledge, is omni (all) benevolent (good), and is eternal in nature (not bound by time).

Keeping these two concepts in mind, here is Alvin Plantinga's structure for the ontological argument:

Premise 1: It is possible that a maximally great being exists.

Premise 2: If it's possible that a maximally great being exists, then a maximally great being exists in some possible world.

Premise 3: If a maximally great being exists in some possible world, then it exists in all possible worlds.

Premise 4: If a maximally great being exists in all possible worlds, then it exists in the actual world.

Premise 5: Therefore, a maximally great being exists in the actual world.

Conclusion: Therefore, God, the maximal being, exists.

It may surprise you that Premises 2 – 5 are fairly noncontroversial. Logically they must be true. The debate is with Premise 1 and whether it's possible for God to exist in some world. The atheist must argue that it's logically impossible for God to exist in any world, just as it's impossible for square triangles to exist. If it's possible that God exists in any world, He must exist in the actual world, which concludes that God exists.

Why, though? Why does this maximally great being have to exist in all worlds? Simple! A maximally great being can't be confined to one world; by definition, maximal greatness would be maximally great in all worlds.

Atheists try to parody this argument in order to manipulate it as a trick that is not logically sound, but their attempts constantly fall short. Atheist philosophers will say, *"Imagine a great island, the greatest island possible, therefore the island exists!"* Initially, people might think there is weight to this argument, but it's quite inconsistent. Any parody uses the natural material world to make the parody – an island, for example. But maximal greatness can't be constrained to the world or nature, because one could always add another palm tree or hula dance to the island in order to make it better. The only way to get maximal greatness is a timeless, infinite, personal being (maximal greatness must be linked to goodness and personhood), and God is the only option.

Finally, there is only one possible maximally great being, because maximal greatness includes infinite power and control, which can only be held by one maximally great being. Two beings cannot each possess infinite power. Two cannot be in control of all things, so there can only be one God – one maximally great being.

If you struggled with understanding this argument, try re-reading the section, or progress to the next one. If it made sense to you, I hope you see how God is not only possible, but indeed a necessary being. If it's even possible God could exist, He does.

Axiological Evidence for God

The term axiological is a fancy way of saying morality. The axiological evidence is the classical moral argument for the existence of God. The moral argument appeals to an innate sense of right and wrong that the Bible claims is written on the hearts of mankind (Romans 2:12-16).

Before going further, we need to define two words: *subjective* and *objective*.

Subjective Moral Values:

Morality that is decided by a specific person or culture but is subject to change with time and culture.

Objective Moral Values:

Morality that is always the case, can never change, and applies to all people at all times.

Subjective is individual opinion, while objective would claim certain things are right and wrong no matter what people think. Subjective would be saying, *"I prefer this flavor of ice cream"*, while objective would be to say, *"One plus one always equals two"*.

Here is the simple structure of the axiological argument for God's existence:

Premise 1: If God does not exist, objective moral values do not exist.

Premise 2: Objective moral values do exist.

Conclusion: Therefore, God exists.

Many in our world today identify themselves as relativists, claiming individuals and cultures decide what is right or wrong for themselves. But is there reason to believe morality is objective in nature? Here is why each premise should be accepted.

Defense of Premise 1: In order for objective standards to exist, there must be a timeless, unchanging standard on which moral codes are based. That standard needs to be outside our universe to be truly objective, because if it's within our universe, it's subject to change. Finally, the standard must be personal in nature, because morality is always interwoven with personhood and about personhood. One author gives the following defense for why the standard for objective morality must be personal:

"Now one may wonder: Why do you actually need a moral law giver if you have a moral law? The answer is

because the questioner and the issue he questions always involves the essential value of a person. You can never talk of morality in abstraction. Persons are implicit to the question and the object of the question. In a nutshell, positing a moral law without a moral law giver would be equivalent to raising the question of evil without a questioner. So you cannot have a moral law unless the moral law itself is intrinsically woven into personhood, which means it demands an intrinsically worthy person if the moral law itself is valued. And that person can only be God."

God is the only possible timeless, unchanging, personal standard that is beyond our universe. Premise 1 should be accepted.

Defense of Premise 2: The defense of this premise is the most experience- or human intuition- based of the evidences. But again, that is what one would expect if the Bible is true and God has written the law on our hearts and given us a sense of right and wrong. As we explore this premise, please understand that extremes must be used to make the point as clear as possible. You must decide for yourself if you believe this to be true.

Objective morality, which requires God, states raping a child or murdering an innocent person is just as wrong as insisting one plus one is three. Raping a child is not a preference of right and wrong; it's not merely based on a culture but is a violation of the moral law that governs mankind. If one rejects objective moral absolutes and standards, he must maintain that, while raping children or putting Jews in gas chambers during the Holocaust was wrong in his own opinion, it can't be said that it's wrong for other people to do it – simply that it's not right for him.

If Hitler was wrong in murdering six million Jews in concentration camps, objective morality must exist. You decide as the reader: was that wrong? If someone walks into an elementary school and murders a dozen children, is that wrong? Or is it just not something you'd choose to do?

Most people intuitively know these things are evil and egregious. While cultures may disagree on some things, there are certain things that are wrong even if an entire group thinks they are permissible. Atheists often use the existence of these evil things to argue an all-powerful and good God doesn't exist, but that line of reasoning actually admits certain things are right or wrong, good or evil, proving the existence of God.

C.S. Lewis, author of <u>The Chronicles of Narnia</u> and other books, was actually converted to Christianity on this argument. C.S. Lewis said:

"My argument against God was that the universe seemed so cruel and unjust. But how had I got this idea of just and unjust? A man does not call a line crooked unless he has some idea of a straight line. What was I comparing this universe with when I called it unjust? If the whole show was bad and senseless from A to Z, so to speak, why did I, who was supposed to be part of the

*show, find myself in such a violent reaction against it?...
Of course, I could have given up my idea of justice by
saying it was nothing but a private idea of my own. But
if I did that, then my argument against God collapsed
too--for the argument depended on saying the world
was really unjust, not simply that it did not happen to
please my fancies. Thus, in the very act of trying to prove
that God did not exist - in other words, that the whole
of reality was senseless - I found I was forced to assume
that one part of reality - namely my idea of justice - was
full of sense. If the whole universe has no meaning, we
should never have found out that it has no meaning: just
as, if there were no light in the universe and therefore no
creatures with eyes, we should never have known it was
dark. Dark would be without meaning."*

If objective morality exists, God is the only possible
source for it, and therefore God exists.

The Desire of God in John 15

By Johnathan Coker

John 15 is one of the most important sections in the Bible. Although at first glance John 15 may seem like a series of disconnected ideas, Jesus is highlighting a few themes that are intensely interlinked. We are first commanded to love one another, and then told that as we grow in that love, we will suffer persecution for the sake of His name. Jesus also gives us helpful hints as to how we are to participate in His love and handle the resulting persecution. It is my view that Jesus's priority is establishing a people who thoroughly and actively display the love of God to and through one another as they engage in friendship with Him.

One of Jesus's main themes in John 15:12-27 is the theme of the second commandment. We are commanded to "love one another as I have loved you" (John 15:12 ESV). From this, we can see that the love Jesus wants us to have is more than a typical friendship; it is something that represents His very person. In order to understand it, we must first understand how Jesus loves us, which we see in John 15:9, "In the same way the Father loves the Son, so have I loved you."

That is intense! I am supposed to love that person who gets on my nerves, that one who always does that thing in the middle of service, or my roommate who never cleans the dishes. It is also that kid who always gets on my nerves and is always getting into trouble, which could be one of my friend's kids or eventually, even my own child. Jesus takes this further in John 15:13 by describing the kind of love He is talking about. It is the kind that continues to love despite the personal cost, even to the death. He desires a people who display this kind of love, because it is the very love He has for us: a kind of love that holds nothing back.

Another major theme highlighted by Jesus in John 15:12-27 is the theme of heroic love in the midst of intense hatred. This love is not merely a love for one's enemies, but a fellowship with Jesus in the midst of His suffering. In John 15:18, we see that the world will hate us because it first hated Him. In John 15:21, we see that this suffering and persecutions happen for the sake of His name. As we grow in love for one another and in likeness to God, we will encounter persecution. As

John 3:19 states, "And this is the judgment: the light has come into the world, and people loved the darkness rather than the light because their works were evil" (John 3:19 ESV).

Further, in Matthew 5 Jesus states, "But I say to you, love your enemies and pray for those who persecute you, so that you may be sons of your Father who is in heaven. For he makes his sun rise on the evil and on the good, and sends rain on the just and on the unjust" (Mathew 5:44-45 ESV). There is a fellowship of His sufferings that we must partake in for the sake of His name while we are on the earth. He desires a people who do not run from suffering in order that the world might know the kind of God He is.

Both of these intense realities leave us with a question: how are we supposed to go about doing these two things? Loving your brother is hard enough, but Jesus expects us to display the same love to our foes and not be angry or shocked when they keep persecuting us.

Thankfully, I believe Jesus gives us the answer right in the passage in John 15:14, "You are my friends if you do what I command you." Friendship with God is the answer. This is how we love another and stand in the face of persecution. This friendship is our anchor in the waves.

John 15:9 is the truth of how we must lean in, because we cannot do John 15:12 or Mathew 5:44 without it. Ultimately, this comes down to asking the

Father to help us with this, as this prayer in friendship with Jesus is the only way to be steady in the coming storm. Therefore, the answer is both incredibly simple and emotionally difficult. We need to ask God to help us to abide in His love that we might be a people who shares His love, even in the midst of trial and persecution.

Ultimately, Jesus wants a people who can display the same love that He has for them. This is why throughout John 15, he emphasizes abiding in His love, and loving others from that. Jesus's final point in John 15 was originally about the apostles, but I think it is apt for us today as well: "And you also will bear witness, because you have been with me from the beginning" (John 15:27). Jesus is after us bearing witness to His name and His identity together as we corporately behold His eternal beauty and majesty. This is the desire of the Godhead: A witness from every tribe and tongue telling of the name, love, and the worth of who God really is.

Slavery and the Bible

By Quin Friberg

The books of history are filled with the ugly truth that human beings can be cruel to each other. Millions have fought and died over the practice of slavery, and both sides have attempted to use the Bible to support their position. Early in the history of America (and almost every other nation in the world), slaves were imported to be bought and sold as property. Many of these slaves were captured from their homes, often in Africa, and many died en route to be sold in foreign lands. Other slaves throughout history were gained through conquering neighboring empires and taking the spoils of war, including slaves. In first-century Rome, many historians believe around 35% of the empire were slaves to the other 65%, which calculates to millions of slaves in ancient Italy alone.

The question is rightfully asked by the skeptic and believer alike, "Why would God allow slavery throughout the Old Testament in Israel, and why would God not condemn such a prevalent practice as slavery in the New Testament, which is set in the slave-filled Roman Empire?" Wouldn't a loving God condemn slavery and support freedom for all men? Why would God choose to ban shellfish under the Jewish law but not slavery? How can Christians say God is moral if He condones this practice?

The Scriptural Debate

As stated previously, people on both sides of the slavery debate used Scripture, both in early America and other times in history, to support their view. Following are the passages often cited by those who see Scripture supporting the practice:

> 1 Peter 2:18: "Servants, be submissive to your masters with all fear, not only to the good and gentle, but also to the harsh."

Why would God tell servants (slaves) to submit to their masters if His plan was for them to be free? Doesn't that command, in essence, show God supports the institution of slavery, even in the New Testament era? Listen to how one skeptic put it when addressing the issue of slavery:

> "It was the Old and New Testaments of the Bible that were the authority for keeping humanity

in serfdom for centuries and for legitimizing slavery in America, making a bloody civil war necessary to give slaves human rights under our Constitution." Ruth Green, 1979, p. 351

Was the Bible really to blame, or do the pages of Scripture oppose those wanting to own slaves? Here are a few examples of the popular passages used to condemn the owning of slaves:

Galatians 3:28: "There is neither Jew nor Greek, there is neither slave nor free, there is neither male nor female; for you are all one in Christ Jesus."

Matthew 7:12: "Therefore, whatever you want men to do to you, do also to them, for this is the Law and the Prophets."

God said all are one in Christ, equal before God, created in His image and valuable to Him. How could anyone reading those verses support slavery? Furthermore, Scripture says to treat other people the way you want to be treated, and no one wants to be kidnapped and sold into slavery, which means no one should do that to another. What then is the biblical position on slavery? Why is there so much confusion regarding the passages? Greg Carey said the following about biblical slavery:

"Don't let anybody tell you that biblical slavery was somehow less brutal than slavery in the United States. Without exception, biblical societies were slaveholding societies."

While skeptics claim there is no difference between

the slavery seen in early America and Old Testament slavery, they are in error. The reason many people use the Bible to support slavery is ignorance (often willful) of the context of the verses. The type of slavery seen in early America and in many parts of the world throughout history and still today, sadly, is soundly rejected in the Bible. How then are the verses to be understood? How is slavery in the Bible different than early American slavery? How could an all-loving God condone such a practice? Here are a few things to keep in mind.

First, not everything that takes place in the Old Testament is the perfect will of God. God created the world perfect and without sin and, in that environment, no form of slavery would ever be necessary. However, sin entered the picture and people began to act wickedly, resulting in God's Old Testament regulations to govern His people, Israel. The same concept would hold true on the topic of divorce. Jesus says in Matthew 19 that God allowed divorce because the hearts of His people were sinful and hard, but in His perfect plan, divorce would never be acceptable. Now granted, there are still rules on divorce, and it's only allowed in very specific circumstances, as it is with slavery.

Next, God has always been consistent in commanding His people to love their neighbor and treat others the way we want to be treated. Many see a loving God as a New Testament idea, and they believe the God of the Old Testament is different. Nothing is further from the truth. God has been consistent and the same throughout history. From the beginning of Scripture, God has commanded loving others:

Leviticus 19:18: "You shall not take vengeance, nor bear any grudge against the children of your people, but you shall love your neighbor as yourself: I am the Lord."

"Neighbor" does not describe only fellow Jews, but the nations surrounding them and foreigners who passed through their land. But wait! Didn't Israel conquer their neighbors and take many of them as slaves? No, they didn't conquer all of them, and when they did take slaves, it was God using them to bring justice in the world. Outside of God using them to bring His justice, they were commanded to love their neighbors. God has always told His people to love and care for others, which is actually seen in His commands regarding slavery.

Old Testament Slaver

God tells His people to love others throughout the pages of Scripture, but the question has to be asked: when dealing with a nation (Israel), what should be done about those who break the law, steal from others, and don't repay their debts, or those who were enemies of Israel and were conquered? Today, those individuals would simply be tossed in prison for years, those who are stolen from often lose their money, and those who loan money often never get it back.

Was it wrong for God to use Israel when enforcing His moral law? Is it wrong for the government to punish those who steal money from another? Is it wrong for the government to punish someone for being an enemy of the state? Doesn't this take place still today in practically every nation on earth? Slavery in Israel was the equivalent of our modern-day prison system. Instead of putting someone who stole or owed money in prison, instead of bankruptcy and jail time to solve the problems, they would become slaves and work for the person they owed to pay off the debt.

Those who were enemies of the state, instead of being religated to prisoner-of-war camps, were allowed to live among the Israelites as their servants, which is far more humane than locking them up for life. Actually, one could argue prison is far more oppressive than slavery in the Bible, yet most people agree there are appropriate times for people to go to prison. Unlike prisons around the world today, slavery in the Bible was designed not simply for the sake of punishment, but for restoration. Debt slaves, those who had borrowed and did not return the money, or those who stole from others, were the largest category of slaves (or servants as many translations render the word), and their time as servants was limited:

> Exodus 22:1-3: "If a man steals an ox or a sheep, and slaughters it or sells it, he shall restore five oxen for an ox and four sheep for a sheep. If the thief is found breaking in, and he is struck so that he dies, there shall be no guilt for his bloodshed. If the sun has risen on him, there shall be guilt for his bloodshed. He should make full restitution; if he has nothing, then he shall be sold for his theft."

Those who stole in Israel were expected to repay (with extra) what was stolen, and if they could not, they must become servants and work until the money was returned. Why would anyone see this as a bad practice? Wouldn't an institution that allowed someone to work and pay off their debt of theft be the ideal situation? Certainly. There is nothing immoral about the system God allowed in Israel to deal with criminals.

Thieves and debtors were not the only slaves, though. The Israelites also made their enemies slaves after conquering them, which many skeptics claim is wrong. However, God is the universal judge and has every right to use Israel to bring judgment upon pagan nations surrounding them. Keep in mind, these are the nations who sacrificed their children in fire, among other horrendous acts. While God brought judgment, He also showed His mercy by allowing many of them to continue living in Israel, which could easily result in their hearing about God and gaining eternal life.

The word "slave" in the Old Testament Hebrew is translated both servant and slave, and can refer to voluntary (yes, you read that right) or involuntary servanthood. While today the term is associated with the atrocities of the slave trade, it didn't always have a negative connotation. The word applies to many revered men in the Old Testament, such as Moses, who was God's servant, Joseph, who was the head of Potiphar's house and possessions, and Eliezer, Abraham's head slave/servant, who ruled over all he had. One of the oldest books, if not the oldest book in the Bible, tells about how servants should be treated:

Job 31:13-15: "If I have despised the cause of my

male or female servant when they complained against me, what then shall I do when God rises up? When He punishes, how shall I answer Him? Did not He who made me in the womb make them? Did not the same One fashion us in the womb?"

Those who compare biblical slavery to the slave trade in early America are ignorant of many verses explaining and clarifying the purpose and treatment of servants. Job makes it clear the one who made him is the same one who made his servants, and God will hold him accountable for how he treats them. Actually, Job says God will punish those who mistreat their servants, which is completely different from the idea that they are property and possessions of their master.

The servant and master relationship condoned by God in the Bible is completely different than our modern-day perception of slavery. Once again, the head servant of Abraham, Eliezer, was considered by Abraham as being his son. Eliezer didn't want to escape being Abraham's slave. Actually, the Old Testament states many slaves chose to stay with their masters, even when their debts were paid off and freedom was theirs:

Deuteronomy 15:16-17: "And if it happens that he says to you, 'I will not go away from you,' because he loves you and your house, since he prospers with you, then you shall take an awl and thrust it through his ear to the door, and he shall be your servant forever. Also to your female servant you shall do likewise."

Servants often became part of the family and chose to stay with their master's household, because they loved them and were provided for by them. Those servants who chose to stay would pierce their ear to signify their choice. Why would someone choose to stay as a servant? Wouldn't everyone want to just escape and get "free" at first chance? Again, many of the slaves were essentially employees, who began their work because of a debt or theft, and often chose to stay and work because their master would provide remuneration for their labor, nothing like the slavery in America.

The Biblical View on Old Testament Slavery

If you're not already convinced biblical servant-hood is different from the early American slave trade, here are eight things the Bible says about slavery to further make the point. Keep in mind, not every verse on slavery can be addressed in one article, but the differences between other types of slavery can be easily shown.

1. Both Servant and Master Benefited

Those in slavery often owed money to someone and becoming a servant allowed them to work and pay off the debt they owed. Servants often worked for someone to whom they weren't indebted, and from their wages, they were able to pay off the one they did owe. Working for someone else to repay a debt could prevent the master from treating the slave poorly, which could happen if the master were the one who was wronged by the slave. Fundamentally, masters were businessmen or family men who needed extra help and would pay off their servant's debt in return for labor. Keep in mind, the servant often chose to stay with the master and continue working, essentially making it an employee-employer relationship.

2. If Masters Abuse Their Slaves, Their Slaves Can Legally Run Away

Deuteronomy 23:15-16: "You shall not give back to his master the slave who has escaped from his master to you. He may dwell with you in your midst, in the place which he chooses within one of your gates, where it seems best to him; you shall not oppress him."

Slaves did have freedom to choose a master who would not abuse them, which would ensure they would be treated well. Once again, this is nothing like slavery around the world throughout history. God would not allow the abusive, immoral practice that many other nations bought into.

3. The "Slave Trade" Was Illegal

Remember, almost all slavery throughout history was built on the foundation of kidnapping someone and selling them for a profit, which is staunchly rejected by God in the Old Testament:

Exodus 21:16: "He who kidnaps a man and sells him, or if he is found in his hand, shall surely be put to death."

God not only forbade the slave trade, there was a death penalty for anyone who participated in it. One can easily argue using this verse that God specifically condemns the slave practices in early America and around the world throughout history, and gave the worst penalty the state of Israel could enact: the death penalty.

4. Nothing to do With Race/Skin

Another way biblical slavery is set apart from other forms of slavery has to do with the racist justifications to which many other forms of slavery appeal. Biblical slavery had nothing to do with skin color. It instead had everything to do with justice, punishment, and restoration:

> Leviticus 19:34: "The stranger who dwells among you shall be to you as one born among you, and you shall love him as yourself; for you were strangers in the land of Egypt: I *am* the Lord your God."

Keep in mind that the Israelites were slaves in Egypt for hundreds of years, and God constantly used that situation to remind them how to treat others. While they were in Egypt, they wanted to be treated well by the Egyptians, and God expected them to treat the foreigner well, too. Many other verses discuss how the Israelites should treat foreigners:

> Deuteronomy 10:17-19: "For the Lord your God *is* God of gods and Lord of lords, the great God, mighty and awesome, who shows no partiality nor takes a bribe. He administers justice for the fatherless and the widow, and loves the stranger, giving him food and clothing. Therefore love

the stranger, for you were strangers in the land of Egypt."

Skin color had nothing to do with slavery in the Bible. God's Word is clear that everyone is part of the same race, the human race, and mistreating people because of their skin color is sinful and wrong:

Acts 17:26: "And He has made from one blood every nation of men to dwell on all the face of the earth, and has determined their preappointed times and the boundaries of their dwellings."

Everyone ultimately comes from Adam and Eve. We're all from the same blood and the same ancestors, and how we treat each other should reflect that truth. God decides which family, country, culture, and skin color someone will be born into, and none of those things should change the way we love and treat each other.

5. Slaves Received Sabbath Rest

The Jews had a one-day weekend, the Sabbath, which was a time when no work could be done, a day set aside for rest and for God. One would think if slavery in the Bible is the same as other parts of the world, their slaves would not have the same "rights" to a break as everyone else, but they did:

Exodus 20:10: "But the seventh day *is* the Sabbath of the Lord your God. *In it* you shall do no work: you, nor your son, nor your daughter, nor your male servant, nor your female servant, nor your cattle, nor your stranger who *is* within your gates."

The command to allow rest for your servant on the Sabbath was written by God in the Ten Commandments themselves, showing once again the extreme differences between Old Testament slavery and other forms. Slaves were also allowed to take part in festivals throughout the year, according to Deuteronomy 16:9-17, again showing how they were treated as human beings, not property.

6. Slaves Received Freedom in the Year of Jubilee

One fascinating tradition commanded by God in the Old Testament was a Jubilee year, which took place every fifty years. At this special time, freedom was given to slaves in Israel:

Leviticus 25:8-13: "And you shall count seven sabbaths of years for yourself, seven times seven years; and the time of the seven sabbaths of years shall be to you forty-nine years. Then you shall cause the trumpet of the Jubilee to sound on the tenth day of the seventh month; on the Day of Atonement you shall make the trumpet to sound throughout all your land. And you shall consecrate the fiftieth year, and proclaim liberty throughout all the land to all its inhabitants. It shall be a Jubilee for you; and each of you shall return to his possession, and each of you shall return to his family. That fiftieth year shall be a Jubilee to you; in it you shall neither sow nor reap what grows of its own accord, nor gather the grapes of your untended vine. For it is the Jubilee; it shall be holy to you; you shall eat its produce from the field. In this Year of Jubilee, each of you shall return to his possession."

The freedom given on the Jubilee year would

prevent generations from being enslaved, which was the case in many other forms of slavery. No family could be enslaved for multiple generations, unless they chose to stay with their master's family, which we discussed earlier.

7. A Master Who Beat His Slave to Death Was Executed

Another regulation showing God's care for those working to pay off debt and the captured enemies of Israel made into servants was the harsh punishment for any master who beat his slave to death:

> Exodus 21:20: "And if a man beats his male or female servant with a rod, so that he dies under his hand, he shall surely be punished."

No one would harshly beat their servants, because if they accidentally killed them, they would be put to death. God made it clear the life of a servant was as equally valuable as the life of a master, and if a master took his servant's life, the punishment was death.

Now, many look at the verse above and claim it does allow masters to beat their slaves, just not to death. They are correct—If a servant was being disruptive, stealing, or hurting the master's family or property. Masters were then allowed to punish their servants, although it wasn't common.

8. Beating Often Resulted in Freedom of the Slave

Although disciplining servants was allowed when they were harming family, being disruptive, destroying property, etc., the practice would be scarce.

> Exodus 21:26-27: "If a man strikes the eye of his male or female servant, and destroys it, he shall let him go free for the sake of his eye. And if he knocks out the tooth of his male or female servant, he shall let him go free for the sake of his tooth."

Why is striking the eyes of your servant specified by God as being wrong? Because the pagan nations around Israel would often gouge the eye(s) out of their servants to punish and hurt them. God says if anyone copies those pagan nations in their horrendous treatment of their slaves, the slave can go free at the master's expense. God didn't stop there, He also said that if a master knocked a tooth out of their servant's mouth, the servant was free to go. Knocking teeth out is not terribly hard, which means no master would risk the expense by beating his servant in a harsh way. God made sure even slaves and servants, who were rightfully paying off debt or being punished for fighting against Israel, were cared for and protected by Jewish law.

Keep in mind, not every passage dealing with slavery can be addressed in one article, and if another passage causes concern, take the time to research the meaning and context.

Let's look at one final consideration on Old Testament slavery. While many of these eight points apply to both foreign enemy servants and Jewish servants, a few apply only to the Jewish debt servant.

Either way, God set up a system superior to our modern-day criminal justice system both in America and in many other parts of the world. Those who did horrible crimes, such as murder, were punished immediately, and those who committed lesser crimes, such as stealing or not returning money, were given the opportunity to repay and clear their crime, something our modern-day system doesn't allow.

Slavery in the New Testament

Critics complain that in the New Testament, God did not condemn the slavery practiced in the Roman Empire at that time. Critics also object to the New Testament's instruction for servants to obey their masters, which in a way supports slavery:

> Colossians 3:22: "Bondservants, obey in all things your masters according to the flesh, not with eye service, as men-pleasers, but in sincerity of heart, fearing God."

Why would God tell His people to obey their masters? Why not tell them slavery is wrong and should be abolished? Why not tell masters who claim to be Christians to free their servants? Consider these following six points as a response to these questions.

1. Many of these New Testament Slave Practices are Similar to the Old Testament Ones Discussed Earlier

Many of the slaves in Rome (and other parts of the world) were debt servants working to pay off a theft or debt owed to another.

2. Lack of Condemnation in a Verse isn't Condoning the Action of Slavery

Take for example, one of the most popular verses in Scripture, which tells followers of Christ how to treat those who mock them:

> Matthew 5:39: "But I tell you not to resist an evil person. But whoever slaps you on your right cheek, turn the other to him also."

God is not saying slapping someone (which was an issue of disrespect, not assault) is right. He simply tells His followers how to respond in light of being wronged. God wants His followers to not return evil for evil, but to return good when evil is received. Just because God tells servants to obey their masters and work hard doesn't mean slavery has His support; it means God wants us to honor Him no matter the circumstances.

3. Biblical Principles do Reject Most Forms of Slavery

God tells His followers to treat others the way they want to be treatedd, which means many forms of slavery are rejected by God: Matthew 7:12: "Therefore, whatever you want men to do to you, do also to them, for this is the Law and the Prophets."

Actually, there is an entire New Testament book dedicated to a story of a slave who ran from his master and then became a follower of Christ. The book of Philemon in the New Testament is short but profound in addressing how Christians should treat their servants. God tells Philemon (through a letter from Paul the apostle) to treat his run-away servant (Onesimus) as a brother in the Lord when he returned, which was completely opposite of the culture which said run-away slaves should be punished.

4. Slave Trading is Directly Rejected Through Scripture

Not only does the Old Testament reject the slave trade and put the penalty of death on those who partake in the evil act, the New Testament condemns treating people as property and capturing people to sell as slaves:

> 1 Timothy 1:9-10 (ESV): "Understanding this, that the law is not laid down for the just but for the lawless and disobedient, for the ungodly and sinners, for the unholy and profane, for those who strike their fathers and mothers, for murderers, the sexually immoral, men who practice homosexuality, enslavers, liars, perjurers, and whatever else is contrary to sound doctrine."

Clearly stated in the list of sins is the enslaving of fellow humans (other versions say kidnap), showing once again God does not support typical slavery. Humans have value in the eyes of God, and while justice at times results in the punishment of those who've committed crimes, God makes sure servants are treated justly as fellow humans, not as property.

5. The Bible Takes an Eternal Perspective

Finally, it should be understood that the Bible, especially the New Testament in presenting the gospel, takes an eternal perspective:

Romans 6:16-18: "Do you not know that to whom you present yourselves slaves to obey, you are that one's slaves whom you obey, whether of sin leading to death, or of obedience leading to righteousness? But God be thanked that though you were slaves of sin, yet you obeyed from the heart that form of doctrine to which you were delivered. And having been set free from sin, you became slaves of righteousness."

God is far more concerned with mankind being slaves of sin, lost and on our way to judgment. Jesus came and died on the cross not to give us earthly freedom, but to save us for all of eternity. In the end, everyone will be a slave to something, and God says the choice is sin or righteousness. Being slaves to sin results in death and judgment, and sadly many have chosen this path. Thankfully, God made a way for sin to no longer have control over us. Through the power of the cross anyone who turns to Jesus can become a slave to righteousness, which leads to life.

The Reason to Pray

By Johnathan Coker

Why do we pray? Is prayer even biblical? Where is prayer found in the Bible? How long should we pray? These questions, among others, have plagued Christians for centuries. As part of what has been termed "the global prayer movement," I have heard many different arguments around the why of corporate prayer. Although these arguments are good for a time, they fail to sustain in the midst of pressure, difficulty, and the questions that arise due to what it means to live for Jesus on this side of eternity.

Although I am far from understanding fully the heart of God on corporate prayer, I believe there is enough evidence to suggest this is God's desire for the church. In this paper, I hope to convince you that not only is corporate prayer biblical, it is God's primary means to partner with the church to bring His kingdom to the earth.

Before going into my personal theology of prayer, it would help to understand what "the global prayer movement" is. It is a global prayer phenomenon, which has brought a surprising new emphasis on prayer into the Body of Christ over the past 40 or so years. Steve Hawthorne comments, "...in recent years so many prayer events are taking place that it is nearly impossible to keep track of all the meetings, prayer watches, initiatives, fasts, and solemn assemblies in just one country or region. National and global prayer initiatives are now commonplace."[1] He further states that, "More than 200 million believers pray every day for the advancement of world missions."[2] This article was written over 10 years ago, and these trends have only continued to grow. Therefore, it is fair to say that the Lord is doing something related to corporate prayer across the earth.

Being a part of something so unique and interesting is amazing, but it can leave one with a fundamental problem: it is so easy to just get caught up in what is happening without asking the difficult questions. It is easy to just re-quote passage after passage without asking if what we are doing even biblical. Many are afraid to ask this question, because, to be perfectly honest, they have this secret fear inside of them that they are wasting their lives on something that doesn't matter as much as missions or being a pastor.

We say we value prayer, but secretly we despise the smallness of our efforts and how others view them. In doing so, we fail to even address our own unbelief and issues on the subject. We are secretly afraid that we will be unable to defend our position with scripture, in-spite of how incredible the swirl is around us.

When I began my own prayer journey two years ago, I found myself in this very position. As one who grew up on corporate prayer, I found myself convinced that this was the Lord's will, without being able to defend my position with Scripture as well as I would like. Sure, I could quote scriptures, but I still failed to truly wrestle with the questions. However, it is important that we understand and ask these difficult questions in order for us to give an answer to anyone who asks in the moment of trial.[3] So, let us ask the question: Is corporate prayer found in the scriptures? The answer is yes, but it is helpful to dive into the specifics.

The biblical foundations of corporate prayer are fascinating. Prayer did not begin with asking God for things, but rather as a conversation with the living God in the Garden of Eden. Some have debated the claim that this was the first instance of prayer, or that Eden was some sort of major worship center, but it is clear that some kind of beholding and worship of the Creator was going on. As Samuel Whitfield argues in *Discipleship Begins with Beholding*, "From the beginning, the Bible presents humanity as a priestly creature who lives in a garden and has unique access to the presence of God."[4]

As Adam and Eve were the first worship leaders, priests, and missionaries,[5] it was their job as images of God to bring heaven, and thus the will of God, to the earth. It is the way God designed the world, and when humanity chose to abandon the will of God, it brought death. Even knowing this, it was still in the heart of God to have a people whose primary mission on the earth was to be His representative, and thus to intercede on His behalf as they beheld and interacted with Him. This was the original purpose of prayer: Corporate interaction with the Creator, fueled by worship to behold him and bring His kingdom to the earth.

The next major instance we see of prayer in the Scripture occurred after the fall, but not before we leave Genesis. After the fall, humanity was broken and scattered. They no longer had direct access to the presence of God, and were consistently dying. Many had left off following the heart of God to pursue their own lusts. As Genesis 6:5 states, "The LORD saw that the wickedness of man was great in the earth, and that every intention of the thoughts of his heart was only evil continually."

However, it is important to note that those who had followed evil were not the only people who were alive on the earth at the time. Genesis 4:26 states, "At that time people began to call upon the name of the LORD." Genesis 5:28-29 gives us more insight, "When Lamech had lived 182 years, he fathered a son and called his name Noah, saying, 'Out of the ground that the LORD has cursed, this one shall bring us relief from our work and from the painful toil of our hands.'" This shadows the Genesis 3:15 promise of one who would end the suffering of humanity. From this, we see that prayer has its roots as early as Genesis 4. Thus, prayer, which we often think of today as asking God to do something, started with asking God to do what He had promised: to end the curse of sin and crush the head of the serpent.

We see prayer in Exodus, and this account gives us even further insight into corporate prayer. In the wake of the terrors of slavery, a cry rose up from the children of Israel: "During those many days the king of Egypt died, and the people of Israel groaned because of their slavery and cried out for help. Their cry for rescue from slavery came up to God. And God heard their groaning, and God remembered his covenant with Abraham, with Isaac, and with Jacob. God saw the people of Israel – and God knew."[6] In the midst of suffering and persecution, a people caught in shame and compromise moved the heart of God through prayer. This prayer brought forth one of the greatest expressions of the power of God in history: the Exodus. We often fixate on the miraculous power of this event and miss the bigger point. The Exodus is not primarily about showing us the miraculous, it is about showing us how God partners with His people to bring about His will on the earth, even though they are in compromise.

Although we typically think of the Moses' argument with Pharoah when we think of Exodus, the majority of the book of Exodus takes place on the mountain of Sinai. From Exodus 19-40, everything that happens is centered on that mountain. This momentary meeting of God and man on the mountain had dramatic implications. As Samuel Whitfield describes, "For the first time in history, an entire corporate people beheld God together...They were gathered to behold the person of God and represent that person to the nations."[7] Further, we see that this is connected to the priesthood and prayer through another verse in Exodus 19, "'You yourselves have seen what I did to the Egyptians, and how I bore you on eagles' wings and brought you to myself. Now therefore, if you will indeed obey my voice and keep my covenant, you shall be my treasured possession among all peoples, for all the earth is mine; and you shall be to me a kingdom of priests and a holy nation.' These are the words that you shall speak to the people of Israel." Therefore, in everything that occurred in the Exodus, God was after a people who were priests. He was after a people who prayed.

Our next and final story in the Bible of corporate prayer is about a little man you may have heard of called David. David sought after God above anything else. As Billy Humphrey states in *Unceasing*, "David's distinguishing attribute is that he prioritized God's presence over all else in his life. That's what it means to be a man after God's own heart – you want God's presence more than you want anything else. His hunger for God's presence catapulted a forgotten shepherd boy from a forgotten town into the role of king over all Israel."[8]

This heart is what led to the most unique moment in his entire reign and in Israel's history as a nation. David literally put the ark of the covenant in a tent and employed people to sing and worship around it. [9] As Fritch says, "...David put the presence of God right at the center of all life and culture. He placed the ark right next to his palace, right in the governmental center of the nation and summoned the nation to honor God night and day."[10] The most unique thing about David, therefore, is how he centered His entire reign and nation around worship and prayer, and how that moved God's heart.

All this leaves us with a lot of interesting stories, but also a question. We can clearly see that corporate worship with prayer has biblical precedent, but is it something God still desires today? Peter addresses this very thing. "As you come to him, a living stone rejected by men but in the sight of God chosen and precious, you yourselves like living stones are being built up as a spiritual house, to be a holy priesthood, to offer spiritual sacrifices acceptable to God through Jesus Christ."[11] He then quotes Exodus 19 to solidify this reality. "But you are a chosen race, a royal priesthood, a holy nation, a people for his own possession, that you may proclaim the excellencies of him who called you out of darkness into his marvelous light. Once you were not a people, but now you are God's people; once you had not received mercy, but now you have received mercy."[12]

We are called to the same realities that Israel was called to in the Exodus. In Isaiah 62:6-7, we are told: "On your walls, O Jerusalem, I have set watchmen; all the day and all the night they shall never be silent. You who put the LORD in remembrance, take no rest, and give him no rest until he establishes Jerusalem and makes it a praise in the earth." Multiple times, Jesus told His disciples to pray. A core part of the Lord's prayer is, "Your will be done, on earth as it is in heaven."[13] Even in Revelation 5, we see that the prayer of the saints are what release God's judgments, just like it was during the Exodus.[14] God's desire has not changed. He still wants a people who represent Him and minister to Him day and night as they wait for Him to appear just like he did in the Exodus.

If all of these things are true, then we know several things that challenge us. We know that God wants us to pray because he wants partnership with humanity. We know that he desires a people who not only pray, but physically represent Him on the earth. We know that He is committed to restoring the earth to the Eden state of beholding and blessing Him.

Yet, prayer remains one of the most resisted things in our lives. We will find any excuse to get away from it, even when we are in a prayer meeting! I cannot recall the number of times in the middle of praying when I have thought, 'Oh, I forgot this thing' or 'I needed to buy this' or any one of a number of distracting thoughts that cloud my head. We are challenged by the truths, yet our prayers are so weak, and our thoughts are filled with every kind of distraction. At other times, we wonder if what we do is even worth it, after all won't someone else do it for us?

One of the most horrifying stories in the whole of human history occurred on the eve of one of the greatest moments of God revealing Himself. As we see in Exodus, "Now Moses used to take the tent and pitch it outside the camp, far off from the camp, and he called it the tent of meeting. And everyone who sought the LORD would go out to the tent of the meeting which was outside the camp. Whenever Moses went out to the tent, all the people would rise up, and each would stand at his tent door, and watch Moses until he had gone into the tent."[15]

The people were content to be near the fire and not actually go to meet with the Lord. We can say the prayers and watch all the sermons and still miss the whole point of why God wants prayer in the first place. It is so easy in an environment like the Western church to push all the responsibility of hearing from God onto one person. I have even found this to be true in small communities. God doesn't want us to be a people who merely say empty prayers filled with meaningless, disconnected words as we watch what God is doing from the sidelines. This is not what God is after. He still wants a people for His own possession who are also priests. He wants transformation through intercession.

As David Thomas states in *Travailing Prayer*, "The Bible Seems utterly unfamiliar with casual prayer: prayer of the mouth and not the heart. Travail – a kind of burdened, focused pressing – seems closer to the throbbing core of prayer in the scripture."[16] Why then, is it so easy for us to become disengaged?

The center-point of the difficulty of prayer comes not only from internal forces, but also external. This is because of the nature of what prayer is. Prayer is asking God to do what He has already said He will do. If there was no opposition to the will of God, then prayer would be viewed for what it really is: the greatest thing in the world. Unfortunately, we live in a world that is surrounded by darkness and have an adversary who is ferociously committed to opposing the will of God on the earth. To top this off, ever since the fall we have had to wrestle against our own flesh, which is itself opposed to God. As James 4:1-3 states, "What causes quarrels and what causes fights among you? Is it not this, that your passions are at war within you? You desire and do not have, so you murder. You covet and cannot obtain, so you fight and quarrel. You do not have, because you do not ask. You ask and do not receive, because you ask wrongly, to spend it on your passions."

There are so many things that are fighting against us praying in the way that God desires, that it is no wonder that every time we begin to pray, we find it so difficult. If God did not desire the person praying to be transformed, then prayer would be difficult enough because of the external forces alone. Because God does desires a people who are like Him in every way, this is made more difficult. We are swimming upstream in the valley against the roaring tide of this age, trying to draw near to the Lord.

How then do we keep praying in the face of such opposition? We all need something that pushes us beyond mere knowledge of the heart of God on prayer into something that sustains us for years to come. That being the case, what is it that sustains prayer? It is the beauty of God. This beauty is what sustained David and pushed him to build the house of the Lord. As the famous verse in Psalms 27:1-4 says, "The LORD is my light and my salvation; whom shall I fear? The LORD is the stronghold of my life; of whom shall I be afraid? When evildoers assail me to eat up my flesh, my adversaries and foes, it is they who stumble and fall. Though an army encamp against me, my heart shall not fear; though war arise against me, yet I will be confident. One thing have I asked of the LORD, that will I seek after: that I may dwell in the house of the LORD all the days of my life, to gaze upon the beauty of the LORD and to inquire in his temple."

God's beauty sustained David through trial. It motivated him to keep reaching for God. As Whitfield describes, "The revelation of the beauty of Jesus has the power to captivate the mind, will, and emotions and produce a people who will endure incredible sacrifices for the sake of His name and His glory."[17]   In *The Call to Day and Night Prayer*, Brad Stroop describes, "The primary purpose and the only needed reason for our worship is because He is worthy. There is nothing to compare Him to and no one in all creation that is as fascinating, as beautiful and majestic and holy. He alone is worthy and His immeasurable worth by itself is reason enough to praise Him."[18] It is His beauty that sustains prayer.

Beauty is also what motivates the end time church. As Whitfield states, "The age will end with a multitude of small church communities, like the church in Antioch, who are worshiping and fasting. They will be captured by the beauty of God, and that will produce an ache – a deep longing – for God to be on the earth again, dwelling among his people as He has promised He will."[19]   That ache is what produces the prayer of the saints that fill the bowls in Revelation 5, ushering in Christ's return. God will continue to pursued a people who long for Him in wholehearted agreement with Him. He longs for a bride who has made herself ready, sustained and fully satisfied by Him, crying out for Him to return.

As Whitfield adds, "Missions exists to produce worship, but in this age, missions also exist to produce David's ache. It exists to produce a people among every people group who will, in the words of Jesus, fast and mourn until He returns."[20] In other words, even missions exist for the sake of producing a ceaselessly praying people.

Over the decades, I have found my journey of prayer has consisted of a series of episodes of the Lord convincing me of its value. At first, I was stubborn and resisted prayer – after all, I wanted to be a pilot! Next, I wanted to do missions and felt the value of prayer was too small to pursue. Why just pray when all the stories about the mission field were so appealing? Eventually, after years of wrestling with the Lord, I joined a local house of prayer, a place dedicated to corporate prayer. After about two years of this, my house of prayer had a chance to pray for some people on the phone. They were rich and were dying of Covid-19 and did not know the Lord. At the time, I thought nothing of it. We were used to praying for people, and although it was a bit different, it was the usual. Overall, it felt so weak.

However, the Lord moved in power and those

people were healed. They set up a meeting with us. They kept telling us through the tears they were shedding, how we had saved their family and all the things they wanted to do for us. The father then told us, "You do not understand how important what it is that you do. Never stop doing this. If you leave, find another place that does this. If there isn't one in the city you go to, build one." After that, I was fully convinced that no matter the size or numbers, God deeply values corporate prayer. An unbeliever understood the value of corporate prayer more than I did. These people have been paying for the rent and building for our house of prayer ever since. What I thought was small, God deeply valued. That which I had secretly despised, He deeply enjoyed.

Going back to the beginning, the reason there is a corporate prayer movement in every nation is God's way of preparing the earth for His return. God so values prayer that He is willing to do anything to prepare a praying people from every nation tribe and tongue who are waiting for His return. Prayer is the most central biblical reality and is the vehicle by which God has drawn people to Himself throughout history. Prayer is about asking God to do what he said He would do. Not matter how many or how few of you there are, God values when you pray together. God loves to reveal Himself to a people who long for Him, and He has created us to be a people who are fueled by His beauty.

Ultimately, intercession is God's means to partner with His people to change the world, literally culminating at the end of the age in bringing heaven to the earth. Even though the journey may be tough and long, ultimately, He is worthy of a people who keep praying and watching. We must take ownership of the call to be the priests of God, no matter what that looks like. I do not want to watch from the sidelines while someone else meets with the Lord. Therefore, I have and will continue to make my mission to watch, pray, and build the house of prayer in partnership with Jesus as I wait and long for Him to return.

Notes:

1 Steve Hawthorne, "The Rise of the Global Prayer Movement," *Prayer Connect* 4, no. 1 (2012): 12.

2 Hawthorne, 11.

3 1 Peter 3:15, *Holy Bible: English Standard Version,* Wheaton, Illinois: Crossway Bibles, 2001.

4 Samuel Whitefield, *Discipleship Begins with Beholding* (Kansas City, MO: OneKing Publishing, 2021), 61-62.

5 Whitfield, 62. Exodus 2:23-25

6 Exodus 2:23-25 ESV

7 Whitfield, *Discipleship Begins with Beholding*, 64

8 Billy Humphrey, *Unceasing: An Introduction to Night & Day Prayer* (Kansas City, MO: Forerunner Publishing, 2015), 32.

9 2 Samuel 6:17-19, 1 Chronicles 16:1-7, 16:37-43, 23:2-5, 25:1-7

10 David Fritch, *Enthroned: Bringing God's Kingdom to Earth Through Unceasing Worship & Prayer* (Burning Ones, 2017), 34.

11 1 Peter 2:4-5 ESV

12 1 Peter 2:9, Exodus 19:6 ESV

13 Matthew 6:13 ESV

14 Revelations 5:8-12 ESV

15   Exodus 33:7-10 ESV

16   David Thomas, *To Sow for a Great Awakening: A Call to Travailing Prayer* (Franklin, TN: Seedbed Publishing, 2016), 12.

17   Whitfield, *Discipleship Begins with Beholding*, 43.

18   Brad Stroup, "Session 2: The Call to Night and Day Prayer," *The Prayer Room Dallas,* Lecture presented at the Culture of Prayer Confrence, October 14, 2022, 4.

19   Whitfield, *Discipleship Begins with Beholding*, 124.

20   Whitfield, 124.

Bibliography

Fritch, David. *Enthroned: Bringing God's Kingdom to Earth Through Unceasing Worship & Prayer.*

>   Burning Ones, 2017.

Hawthorne, Steve. "The Rise of the Global Prayer Movement." *Prayer Connect*, no. 4 (2012). https://www.globalprn. com/wp-content/uploads/The-Rise-of-the-Global-Prayer-Movement- Steve-Hawthorne.pdf.

Holy Bible: English Standard Version. Wheaton, Illinois: Crossway Bibles, 2001.

Благодать вам! Grace to you!

By Charissa Fryberger

Благодать и мир вам от Бога нашего Отца и от Господа Иисуса Христа! *Grace and peace to you from God our Father and the Lord Jesus Christ!*

I often use this phrase from the first chapter of Ephesians to enter into prayer—to find God so I can talk to Him. He opens the conversation, offering me this most precious gift before I can even begin to ask for it. *Grace and peace* from *Him!*

Doing my personal Bible study in both my languages, English and Russian, allows me to see the Scripture from two different translational angles. However, that word for grace, Благодать, (pronounced "blagodot") puzzles me in Russian. It translates as a noun: *grace* to you—some*thing* He is offering. It is a gift generously granted to each of us by the Spirit through the sacrifice of Christ on the cross. It is the what that we need to change the state of our hearts and minds and allows us to sit in His presence, even though we have "sinned against Him in thought, word, and deed by what we have done and by what we have left undone."[1]

However, in Russian, Благодать looks like a verb; "ать" is a verb ending and "дать" is the verb "to give." So, grace in Russian is a noun, but an active, happening noun. In English, I need another word—a verb—in my sentence about grace. I need something for grace to be doing: grace *is* given; grace *flows* from God; grace *covers* our sins; by grace we *are saved* and *are brought* back into relationship with God (and with each other).

Perhaps the Russian is closer to capturing the true essence of grace. Grace (noun) is, but grace also does. It is a living, flowing, healing noun (but since I'm back in English I need all those active "ing" words to say what I'm trying to say).

Perhaps grace should begin with a capital letter and end with a period, serving as both the noun and the verb—a complete sentence in a single word:

Grace.

Notes:
[1] "The General Confession," *The Book of Common Prayer*, 2019.